Taming Globalization

Taming Globalization

Frontiers of Governance

Edited by
David Held and
Mathias Koenig-Archibugi

polity

First published in 2003 by Polity Press in association with Blackwell Publishing Ltd

Editorial office:
Polity Press
65 Bridge Street
Cambridge CB2 1UR, UK

Marketing and production:
Blackwell Publishing Ltd
108 Cowley Road
Oxford OX4 1JF, UK

Distributed in the USA by
Blackwell Publishing Inc.
350 Main Street
Malden, MA 02148, USA

A catalogue record for this book is available from the British Library.

Library of Congress Cataloging-in-Publication Data

Taming globalization : frontiers of governance / edited by David Held and Mathias Koenig-Archibugi.
   p. cm.
Includes bibliographical references and index.
ISBN 0-7456-3076-6 – ISBN 0-7456-3077-4 (pbk.)   1. Globalization.
   2. Globalization – Economic aspects.   I. Held, David.   II. Koenig-Archibugi, Mathias.
JZ1318.T36   2003
303.48′2–dc21   2002153365

Typeset in 11 on 13pt Sabon
by Graphicraft Limited, Hong Kong
Printed and bound in Great Britain by TJ International, Padstow, Cornwall

For further information on Polity, visit our website: www.polity.co.uk

Contents

Contents

Editors' Preface

The chapters of this book (with the exception of the Introduction and chapter 6) are revised versions of the Miliband Lectures on Global Economic Governance given at the London School of Economics and Political Science between January and June 2002. As the organizers of the lectures and the editors of this volume, we have added an introduction and final chapter to help contextualize and round out the arguments.

This series of Miliband Lectures was devoted to one of the crucial questions of our time: the relationship between processes of economic globalization and the conditions of human development, social justice and democratic accountability. We believe that, by exploring this relationship from various perspectives, the lecturers have sketched a powerful agenda for the reform of the existing system of global economic governance, and that their thoughts and recommendations demand a wider public hearing.

The Miliband Lectures honour the memory of Ralph Miliband, who taught at the LSE from 1949 until 1972. His work was dedicated to the study of questions that are very close to the theme of this volume: the relationship between the capitalist economy and democratic governance, the link between economic and political power, and the possibility of a more egalitarian and democratic alternative to the existing world order. As scholars and citizens across the globe debate the nature and consequences of economic globalization, we believe that his concerns are more relevant today than ever.

The Miliband Programme is funded through a generous bequest of a former LSE Ph.D. student, who was inspired by Ralph Miliband's critical vision. This bequest has made the lecture series possible, and we are very grateful to all those who supported our initiative; in particular, we wish to thank Anthony Giddens, Fred Halliday, Henrietta Moore, Marion Kozak, David Miliband and Edward Miliband. We are also grateful to the Global Dimensions Programme, based at the LSE's Centre for the Study of Global Governance, for providing additional resources.

D. H. and M. K.-A.

About the Contributors

Robert E. Goodin is Professor of Social and Political Theory and of Philosophy at the Research School of Social Sciences, Australian National University. He is the Founding Editor of *The Journal of Political Philosophy* and author of many books, including *Protecting the Vulnerable* (1985), *Reasons for Welfare* (1988), *Green Political Theory* (1992), *Utilitarianism as a Public Philosophy* (1995), *Social Welfare as an Individual Responsibility: For and Against*, with David Schmidtz (1998) and *The Real Worlds of Welfare Capitalism*, with B. Headey, R. Muffels and H.-J. Dirven (1999). He has also co-edited major reference books: *A Companion to Contemporary Political Philosophy*, and a follow-up *Contemporary Political Philosophy: An Anthology*, both co-edited with Philip Pettit (1993 and 1997) and *A New Handbook of Political Science*, co-edited with Hans-Dieter Klingemann (1996).

David Held is Graham Wallas Professor of Political Science at the London School of Economics and Political Science. He is the author of *Democracy and the Global Order: From the Modern State to Cosmopolitan Governance* (1995), *Models of Democracy* (second edition, 1996), co-author of *Global Transformations: Politics, Economics and Culture* (1999), and editor or co-editor of *Prospects for Democracy: North, South, East, West* (1993),

About the Contributors

Cosmopolitan Democracy: An Agenda for a New World Order (1995) and *Re-imagining Political Community* (1998).

Robert O. Keohane is James B. Duke Professor of Political Science, Duke University. He is the author of *After Hegemony: Cooperation and Discord in the World Political Economy* (1984), for which he was awarded the second annual Grawemeyer Award in 1989 for Ideas Improving World Order. He is also the author of *International Institutions and State Power: Essays in International Relations Theory* (1989), co-author (with Joseph S. Nye Jr) of *Power and Interdependence: World Politics in Transition* (third edition 2001), and co-author (with Gary King and Sidney Verba) of *Designing Social Inquiry: Scientific Inference in Qualitative Research* (1994). His most recent book is *Power and Governance in a Partially Globalized World* (2002). He was president of the International Studies Association, 1988–9, and the American Political Science Association, 1999–2000.

Mathias Koenig-Archibugi is Research Fellow at the London School of Economics. He is author of articles and book chapters on global governance, international relations theory, the international dimensions of democratization, and European integration in foreign and security policy.

John Gerard Ruggie is the Evron and Jeane Kirkpatrick Professor of International Affairs and Director of the Center for Business and Government at Harvard University's Kennedy School of Government. From 1997 to 2001 he was Assistant Secretary-General and chief adviser for strategic planning to United Nations Secretary-General Kofi Annan. His major responsibilities included designing and managing Kofi Annan's Global Compact, which promotes human rights, labour standards and environmental principles in global corporate practices. He also played a leading role in preparing Annan's celebrated report to the United Nations Millennium Summit, entitled 'We the Peoples: The UN in the 21st Century'.

He has published six books, including *Winning the Peace: America and World Order in the New Era* (1996) and *Constructing the World Polity* (1998). He has provided numerous op-ed and TV commentaries around the world.

Joseph E. Stiglitz is Professor of Economics, Finance and International Affairs at Columbia University. He was awarded the 2001 Nobel Prize in Economics by the Royal Swedish Academy of Sciences. Professor Stiglitz has made contributions to every subfield of economic theory – microeconomics, macroeconomics, industrial organization, international economics, labour economics, financial economics and development economics. He has been a professor at Yale, Princeton, Oxford, and Stanford. He served as chairman in President Clinton's Council of Economic Advisors and later as chief economist of the World Bank.

Robert Hunter Wade is Professor of Political Economy at the London School of Economics. He has taught at Victoria, Sussex, Princeton, MIT, and Brown universities; and has held fellowships at the Institute for Advanced Study (Princeton), the Russell Sage Foundation (New York) and the Institute for Advanced Study (Berlin). In the 1980s he worked as a staff economist at the World Bank, and later as an analyst at the Office of Technology Assessment, an arm of the US Congress. He is the author of *Irrigation and Agricultural Politics in South Korea* (1982), *Village Republics: Economic Conditions of Collective Action in South India* (1988) and *Governing the Market: Economic Theory and the Role of Government in East Asian Industrialization* (1990). The latter won the American Political Science Association's award for Best Book in Political Economy (for the years 1989–91). He wrote a By Invitation essay for *The Economist* on world income distribution, its structure, causes and consequences, and ameliorative international public policies (28 April 2001).

Introduction: Globalization and the Challenge to Governance

Mathias Koenig-Archibugi

During the past decade, 'globalization' has become a lens through which an increasing number of politicians, business people, journalists, scholars and citizens view and make sense of a changing world. Sweatshop workers in Central America, human rights activists in East Timor, entrepreneurs in transition economies, Inuit threatened by global warming in their Arctic homelands, HIV-infected people in Southern Africa, not to mention stockbrokers in London or Tokyo, sense that their fortunes partly depend on events occurring in distant parts of the globe. The notion of 'globalization' provides a shared vocabulary to express this sense of connectedness – although those affected might well have very different views about the word and what it conveys. In fact, depending on the circumstances, some people consider themselves liberated and excited about new opportunities for economic or social advancement, while others may feel increasingly threatened and powerless.

This book aims to explore ways in which the positive sides of globalism can be promoted while its detrimental effects are tamed. The contributors focus on economic globalization and recognize that it could be a force for good, but maintain that this potential can be realized only if market forces are checked and balanced by a political framework capable of ensuring social sustainability and justice.

Mathias Koenig-Archibugi

Globalization as a contested phenomenon

Globalization is not supplanting traditional lines of social conflict and cooperation, but it is redrawing them. Employers and trade unionists, environmentalists and polluters, indigenous peoples and multinational corporations, feminists and male chauvinists, fundamentalists and liberals, free traders and protectionists, human rights activists and authoritarian rulers, nationalists and multilateralists, the 'North' and the 'South': all these groups have found that the capacity to achieve their goals is affected, in one way or another, by the 'forces of globalization'. Consequently many of them seek to make sense of this phenomenon, understand its implications for their interests and values, and sometimes try to influence its further development – or bring it to a halt.

The popularity of the word 'globalization' is partly due to its ambiguity and ability to assume different connotations depending on who is using it in which context. Certainly, economic globalization has many supporters. It is generally defined as the involvement of a growing number of people and countries in multicontinental networks of trade and investment – in what many simply call 'the world market'. Supporters praise globalization because it means that more and more individuals, as consumers and producers, can enjoy the benefits of economic liberalization, competition and innovation. In addition, many of them believe that increasing exposure to transnational flows of communication leads to a better understanding across cultural boundaries and convergence towards 'universal' values, such as freedom, democracy, human rights, and (for some) private economic enterprise.

However, globalization has acquired a quite threatening meaning to many people, in developing countries as well as in the affluent 'North'.[1] This diffidence or outright hostility has many sources. Economic openness exposes workers and firms to unwelcome competition from abroad, and increases the risk that companies will relocate their production elsewhere. Those negatively affected by this can have a direct material interest in opposing globalization. Others are concerned that competition between locations for mobile capital might lead to a race to the bottom in environmental standards. Hostility towards globalization can stem also from an instinctive diffidence vis-à-vis the external world, or the fear that a cherished and distinctive way of life is condemned to disappear as a result of cultural standardization. Among all possible concerns associated with globalization, two seem particularly important from a progressive point of view: the fear that globalization is eroding democratic governance, and the belief that it exacerbates inequality and injustice.

Economic globalization as threat to democratic citizenship

The idea of democratic citizenship implies that the polity is a community of people who exercise self-governance. But in order for this idea to be an approximation of actual democratic practices, the main conditions affecting the social life of the members of the political community need to be under their collective control.[2] The condition of collective autonomy includes the control of the economic sphere: normative conceptions of democratic citizenship assume that economic interactions can be regulated according to the expressed will of the majority, once different political-economic values and policy options have been debated by the citizens or, more plausibly, their representatives.

Of course, this strong ideal of self-governance has never been attained in practice, not least because most polities have been involved in a web of economic, cultural and political interactions that prevented them from being fully autonomous. However, for a few decades after World War II, it seemed that a satisfactory balance between democratic self-governance and international openness could be approached in the rich Western world, at least for the majority of citizens.[3] During the 'Keynesian era', governments and legislatures in advanced capitalist countries enjoyed substantial room for manoeuvre in deciding regulative and redistributive economic and social policies.[4] In this 'Golden Age' of welfare capitalism, investment opportunities for capital owners were largely limited to their national economies, and competition was mainly between companies of the same country. Governments were able to determine the rate of return of financial investment and indirectly of job-creating real investment through their interest rate policies, and their fiscal and spending policies enabled them to influence aggregate domestic demand. This fostered among citizens and their representatives the belief that they could shape the society they lived in according to their social, cultural and ecological preferences, without having to renounce the benefits provided by a dynamic market economy.

After the 1970s, perceptions changed. The dominant view has become that the democratic state is now less able to control capital movements, and that any policy initiative that might affect the rate of return on investment – interest rate policy, taxation, social and ecological regulation – has to be considered carefully in light of the risk of capital flight or reduced inward investment. The mobility of capital, goods, people and pollutants has not been matched by the development of adequate regulative capacities at the international level.[5] As a result of the diverging spatial reaches of economic activity and political control, a divergence which has been accelerating since the 1980s, people are increasingly torn between their role as consumers and investors, who might benefit from globalization because of lower prices, wider choice and better income opportunities, and their role as citizens, which risks becoming less and less meaningful because of the declining opportunity for collective self-governance.

Norberto Bobbio has pointed out that democracy requires that 'those called upon to take decisions, or to elect those who are to take decisions, must be offered real alternatives and be in a position to choose between these alternatives.'[6] Today there is a widespread concern that democracy is being 'hollowed out': formally, democratic institutions and procedures remain in place; substantively, the range of feasible options has shrunk as a result of the constraints imposed by international markets and the investors' threat of 'exit'.[7]

Of course, not everybody agrees that highly mobile economic forces are a problem for democracy. It has been argued that 'in some ways, capital markets, driven by the decisions of millions of investors and borrowers, are highly "democratic". They act like a rolling 24-hour opinion poll. Moreover, they increase politicians' accountability by making voters more aware of governments' performance.'[8] But many people, and not only those the media call anti-globalization activists, would object to such an optimistic conclusion, for at least two reasons. First, because what people want in their specific role as investors might well be at odds with what they want as citizens, that is, when they take into account a broader range of values and interests. Second, the distribution of economic resources among individuals is so unequal that it hardly makes sense to refer to the resulting 'voting power' as democratic. Various authors have shown that the relationship between economic globalization and democracy is likely to be much more problematic than optimists assert.[9]

Globalization as a problem for social justice

Levels of material welfare in different parts of the world are shockingly unequal. Children who are lucky enough to be born in Western Europe have a much higher chance of reaching adulthood than children born in many parts of Africa. A person's opportunity to attain material prosperity and other advantages depends to a significant extent on where he or she happens to live. Many observers would agree that such arbitrariness in the distribution of life chances represents the main ethical problem of our time. However, the link between the inequality of opportunity among different societies and the intensification of global economic relations is controversial. First, it is debated whether global inequality is currently increasing or declining. In this volume, Robert Wade shows that the answer depends on how global inequality is defined and measured. Moreover, it is debated whether the countries that are left behind in terms of economic growth are still poor because of their involvement in international networks of trade and investment, or rather because they are *not* involved enough in the global economy. In other words, is poverty the result of globalization or marginalization? The World Bank and others assert that there is a positive link between a country's integration in world markets and its economic performance – a link that other analysts (see Wade in this volume) have called into question.

Whether globalization exacerbates or decreases inequality *between* countries, on many accounts it impinges on the pursuit of social justice *within* each country. Progressive political forces often adhere to a conception of social justice whose main tenet has been formulated by John Rawls in the following terms: social and economic inequalities are admissible, but only in so far as they are to the greatest benefit of the least advantaged members of society.[10] Under conditions of globalization, safeguarding the well-being of the least well off might require policies that provide increased incentives and remuneration to mobile factors of production (notably capital and highly skilled labour) because their exit or non-entry might damage the country's economic performance and indirectly the most vulnerable members of society. As a result of globalization a government willing to protect the most vulnerable within its jurisdiction may be compelled to tolerate rising levels of inequality among its citizens.[11] Left-of-centre political parties and movements traditionally consider the implementation of egalitarian economic and social policies as the way to enhance fairness, but globalization may call this positive link into question by engendering a tension between the pursuit of equality and the pursuit of justice.[12]

More generally, the net benefits of global economic integration may be positive, but globalization would nevertheless be a disturbing phenomenon if its benefits were distributed unfairly among

those taking part in it. Like most other large-scale social processes, globalization generates losers as well as winners. Often the
losers are those who are already disadvantaged for other reasons.
When this is the case, from an egalitarian point of view economic
globalization can be justified only if these losers are compensated
out of the benefits accruing to the gainers. Yet the possibility of
such compensation is problematic at both the domestic and the
international level. At the domestic level, where the institutions of
the welfare state are traditionally based, the functioning of redistribution mechanisms could be affected by the threat of the exit of
capital and highly skilled labour. The situation is even more problematic at the international level, where the existing mechanisms
for the redistribution of material resources are weaker and less institutionalized than within states, and a major institution-building
effort would be required to set up the necessary capabilities.

Responses to globalization

Before giving an overview of the chapters of this book, it is useful
to consider briefly the existing spectrum of views about the appropriate policy response to globalization. The diversity of views on
this matter has sparked an intense and wide-ranging debate that
forms the background to the contributions in this volume. Broadly
speaking, four different strategies vis-à-vis economic globalization
can be identified, and their respective proponents might be called
sceptics, deregulators, reversers, and internationalists.

Sceptics believe that international economic integration has not
reduced significantly the regulative and redistributive capacities
of states, and therefore that it should not be seen as a real threat
to democratic governance. For some sceptics, the discourse of
globalization is mainly a myth propagated by conservative and
liberal politicians, media and business people in order to present
the dismantling of the welfare state as an objective 'necessity'.
In reality, the sceptics argue, the democratic state is still able to

redistribute wealth, regulate business and set environmental standards. Whether it does or not depends on the balance of power between different interest groups and political parties within each country, rather than on the pressures of the world market.

Deregulators, by contrast, believe that globalization *does* reduce the capacity of governments to determine what happens within their jurisdiction, and they think that this is a beneficial process. Since markets are able to allocate resources more efficiently than governments, any development that limits the ability of governments to intervene in the economy is more likely to be a reason for celebration than concern. In most cases, the best governments can do is to promote 'negative integration' among as many economies as possible, that is, to remove the remaining barriers to the free circulation of goods and capital (and possibly people).

Reversers agree that globalization is constraining public policy making, and precisely for this reason they would like to slow it down or even 'roll it back'. 'Renationalization' is justified as the safest or only way to protect democratic governance, social justice, cultural identity and/or the environment. Some reversers argue that international economic integration is primarily the result of past political choices made by governments (rather than uncontrollable technological progress), and therefore the same governments could choose to restore the importance of national boundaries for economic and social activities.

Finally, *internationalists* argue that the best way to deal with the negative aspects of international economic integration is to make politics as global as the economy. Creating an effective system of global governance would allow the benefits of globalization to be reaped without passively accepting its disadvantages. Of course, internationalists disagree vehemently about how this is to be attained. Some favour cooperation between sovereign states (what Keohane and Nye call the 'club model of multilateral cooperation'),[13] arguing that only governments can have the democratic legitimacy to decide policies at the global level. Others advocate the establishment of a multilayered system of cosmopolitan democracy or even the creation of a world state. Furthermore, some internationalists stress the need to reach beyond public agencies and advocate the close involvement of non-state actors, notably non-governmental organizations (NGOs) and/or companies, in the governance of the global economy. Despite these substantial differences, what unites internationalists is belief in the necessity and feasibility of *positive integration*, that is, the construction of a global regulatory framework that functions at the same level as economic interactions. It is particularly remarkable that a growing number of anti-corporate activists are converging on internationalist positions, as their motto evolves from 'No Global' to 'New Global'.[14]

The chapters in this volume

The contributors to this volume believe that globalization is a real and consequential process. They also believe that it can be reconciled with democratic principles and social justice, but that this reconciliation requires a major effort aimed at the creation of adequate structures of global governance. Robert Wade shows why markets alone cannot be relied upon if the goal is to lift the less advantaged members of world society out of poverty and reduce the massive gap in global incomes. Robert Goodin, Joseph Stiglitz, John Gerard Ruggie, Robert Keohane, and David Held suggest internationalist responses to the challenges that globalization poses to governance.

In chapter 1, Robert Hunter Wade criticizes those strands of market liberalism that credit economic globalization with a diminution of poverty and income inequality on a global scale. He scrutinizes the main source of statistical data on poverty – the studies undertaken by the World Bank – and casts doubts on their reliability, with regard both to their capacity to estimate the absolute number of poor people and their capacity to gauge the direction of poverty trends between the 1980s and the 1990s. Furthermore, he shows that the answer to the question whether global economic inequalities have increased or decreased in the past decades depends on a number of methodological choices for which there is no obvious or invariably 'best' solution. Wade illustrates how alternative measures of income, alternative samples and weightings of countries, and alternative measures of distribution result in different estimates of global income inequality and its trend, and concludes that world income inequality has actually become more severe since the 1970s, according to a plausible approach to its measurement.

Wade also criticizes the contention that 'more globalizing' countries are better at promoting growth and alleviating poverty than 'less globalizing' countries. According to Wade, focusing on the *increase* of a country's involvement in the world economy rather than on its actual *level* masks the fact that several of the most rapidly growing economies did not adopt liberal trade and investment policies. One of the reasons why globalization has done little to reduce poverty and inequality is that open markets do not necessarily generate convergence between low-income zones and high-income zones, due to the tendency of high value-added activities to cluster in specific locations, thus generating network effects and increasing returns to scale. If the market cannot overcome this division, argues Wade, public policies are required to reduce the income gap between the rich and the poor.

Joseph E. Stiglitz argues in chapter 2 that the current system of global governance is heavily biased against developing countries. International institutions such as the International Monetary Fund (IMF) and the World Trade Organization (WTO) are dominated by rich countries, which impose agreements and policies that are often detrimental to the interests of the populations of poorer countries. In international trade negotiations, there are unfair agendas regarding textiles and agricultural goods, intellectual property rights, and trade in services. Moreover, the IMF prescribes policies such as the privatization of social security while proscribing countercyclical policies – the opposite of what developed countries do. Most notably, the IMF has induced developing countries to liberalize their capital markets, and this aggravated the financial crises of the 1990s. Stiglitz argues that the most successful countries of the world have taken part in globalization, but have done so in a selective and controlled way. They have gradually liberalized trade, but were much more cautious when it came to liberalizing capital markets. Countries that liberalized capital markets too quickly, often under pressure from the IMF and the US Treasury, suffered most from the financial crises of the 1990s.

Stiglitz offers a bold programme for reforming global economic governance. He pleads for the inclusion of a broader range of stakeholders in the decision process, for making voting power in the IMF and the World Bank less skewed, for increasing the transparency of decision-making, for changing the approach to crisis management (notably rules on bankruptcy when countries cannot pay their debts), and for extending surveillance to issues such as employment and working conditions. He further argues that more effort should be put into strengthening – rather than undermining – democracy, and on securing adequate resources for financing global public goods.

Robert E. Goodin examines globalization from an ethical point of view, asking how it changes the conditions under which social justice can be pursued. In chapter 3, he argues that some basic human rights have a credible claim to universal application, but that moral universalism does not necessarily rule out particularistic moral relationships. Goodin's version of moral universalism is compatible with the idea that people have special responsibilities to those who are closer to them, and only residual responsibilities to distant strangers. But this means that people lacking effective support from those most responsible for their welfare have the right to receive assistance from the worldwide moral community. This residual duty to supply protection and aid applies most clearly to refugees, but it also has important implications for poor countries whose governments are unable to take care of their populations without external help.

Goodin argues that progressive movements have often adopted a strategy of 'compartmentalized cosmopolitanism', which regards the pursuit of justice 'one country at a time' as the best way to maximize worldwide justice. Because of the ubiquitous economic, political, social and environmental spillovers across borders, as well as the increasing possibility of pursuing justice at a distance, compartmentalized cosmopolitanism is no longer a viable strategy for progressive political forces (if it ever was). According to Goodin, campaigners for social justice should neither resign themselves to the inequities of the global economy nor attempt to wreck it, because good mechanisms for the pursuit of justice on a global scale do exist. He argues that, in addition to multilateral treaties among states and transnational civil society networks, a system of global taxation of financial transactions would be an ethically desirable and politically feasible mechanism for the globalization of justice.

In the early 1980s John Gerard Ruggie introduced into the study of world politics the concept of 'embedded liberalism', which proved highly influential in characterizing the balance between market efficiency and social community that was attained in Western Europe and North America after World War II. The first golden age of international economic integration in the nineteenth century had generated unsustainable social tensions, and the resulting backlash against globalization had pushed most countries towards economic and political nationalism in the 1930s. Postwar leaders in the Western world managed to combine the benefits of economic openness with the development of institutional mechanisms able to compensate market losers for the dislocations generated by economic internationalization.

The current backlash against globalization raises the question of whether a new compromise between market forces and values of social community can be built, this time at the global level. In chapter 4, Ruggie stresses that governance at the global level is not a monopoly of states and that some of the most significant attempts to reconcile corporate goals with social and ecological values result from direct pressure put by civil society organizations on companies. The engagement of civil society with multinational corporations has produced a global public domain, 'an arena of discourse, contestation and action organized around global rule making – a transnational space that is not exclusively inhabited by states'. Ruggie shows that among the most significant results of this global public domain are a great number of 'certification institutions', with codes of conduct being adopted by companies as a response to, and sometimes in association with, civil society organizations. Another significant outcome is the Global Compact, which is a social learning network launched by the UN Secretary-General and which commits the participating companies to promoting core UN principles within corporate domains.

Ruggie does not claim that voluntary initiatives like the Global Compact (which he had a central role in designing and managing) and certification institutions represent a simple solution to governance problems in the global economy, but he shows that they are a worthwhile contribution towards the reconstruction of embedded liberalism at the global level.

Robert O. Keohane advocates the strengthening of multilateral organizations and their capacity to steer globalization towards socially desirable goals. He is sceptical about claims that a universal global society is emerging, that the whole world is adopting a common set of values and rules. While this is arguably occurring in certain regional contexts, such as Western Europe, the persistence of anti-liberal and fundamentalist beliefs among significant sections of the world's population perpetuates a global system that is prone to conflict and violence. In chapter 5, Keohane concludes that a comprehensive system of global governance based on cosmopolitan democracy (see Held in chapter 6) is unattainable for the time being. However, he argues that more limited steps towards making the governance of global issues more accountable are possible. He agrees with the activists in the 'anti-globalization' movement that there are substantial accountability gaps in global governance, but points out that many of their campaigns have focused on the wrong targets, on multilateral organizations. While there is substantial scope for increasing their accountability to a broader range of interests, multilateral organizations should not be the primary target of reformist campaigns, because they are much more open and accountable than other actors in world politics, notably multinational corporations, transgovernmental networks, religious movements and organizations, terrorist networks and, especially, powerful states.

For Keohane, powerful states represent a major source of the accountability deficit of global governance: their rulers might be accountable to their own populations through institutionalized mechanisms of election and control (internal accountability) but they are much less accountable to the broader set of people who are affected by their decisions (external accountability). International organizations represent an important way of putting some constraints on the actions of powerful states, and therefore reformist movements should be careful not to undermine their legitimacy and influence. Keohane warns that weakening these institutions will not stop globalization, but simply allow the strongest actors to exercise their power in a more irresponsible way.

David Held emphasizes that national governments are no longer the only locus of political authority. An increasing number of public and private agencies, at national, regional and global levels, exercise effective power and set norms that regulate distinct areas of human activity. These agencies form a multilayered system of global governance which has a greater capacity to tackle economic, military, political and environmental interdependence than national efforts and policies alone. While governments increasingly realize that certain problems can be solved only through collaborative efforts, the form of cooperation that prevails in most policy domains – executive multilateralism – is still quite inadequate in relation to vital issues such as the gross discrepancy between the malnutrition, disease and illiteracy that is common in many parts of the world and the affluence enjoyed by most people in the industrialized countries.

In chapter 6, Held advocates a shift towards an alternative model of cooperation: cosmopolitan multilateralism. Cosmopolitan morality is based on the principles of equal worth, reciprocal recognition and impartial treatment. These principles are entrenched in important international legal documents, but they are not yet supported by adequate institutional capabilities. Their realization requires the development of a cosmopolitan polity, where authority is located at different levels depending on the degree to which issues stretch across borders and affect different populations. Controversies – including disputes about the appropriate jurisdiction for handling particular issues – would be solved through legalized mechanisms rather than the discretional threat or use of force by powerful states, or by market forces. Held discusses how public deliberation based on cosmopolitan principles might be fostered beyond the nation-state, and proposes a range of institutional reforms involving the establishment of regional and global assemblies, the restructuring of functional intergovernmental organizations, the use of referenda, and the creation of cosmopolitan law-enforcement capabilities.

While not always in agreement on questions of interpretation and prescription, the contributors to this volume all reject both the harshness of unbridled global capitalism and the stifling atmosphere of political and economic nationalism. They also share a commitment to a global governance inspired by cosmopolitan values, and the belief that international institutions are an indispensable means of promoting these values in the global system. This book sets these out in a clear way, thus laying down a progressive agenda for the reform of global governance.

Notes

1   David Held and Anthony McGrew, *Globalization/Anti-Globalization* (Cambridge: Polity, 2002).
2   David Held, *Democracy and the Global Order* (Cambridge: Polity, 1995).

3   John Gerard Ruggie, 'International regimes, transactions and change: embedded liberalism in the postwar economic order', *International Organization*, 36 (spring 1982).

4   Fritz W. Scharpf, *Governing in Europe: Effective and Democratic?* (Oxford: Oxford University Press, 1999), p. 36.

5   David Held, Anthony McGrew, David Goldblatt and Jonathan Perraton, *Global Transformations* (Cambridge: Polity, 1999).

6   Norberto Bobbio, *The Future of Democracy* (Cambridge: Polity, 1987), p. 25.

7   The empirical evidence concerning the shrinking of the range of feasible policies – and specifically the retrenchment of the welfare state – is not clear-cut. Some have argued that the combination of high trade openness and high capital mobility tends to reduce social protection: see for instance Dani Rodrik, *Has Globalization Gone Too Far?* (Washington, DC: Institute for International Economics, 1997). Others have shown that countries with the 'right' political institutions – most notably inclusive electoral institutions and social corporatism – are able to resist the downward pressure of globalization: see Duane Swank, *Global Capital, Political Institutions, and Policy Change in Developed Welfare States* (Cambridge: Cambridge University Press, 2002). Geoffrey Garrett and Deborah Mitchell demonstrate that, in the member countries of the Organization for Economic Cooperation and Development (OECD), greater exposure to international trade (but not foreign direct investment or imports from low-wage countries) corresponds to a less generous welfare state, but the effect is not particularly strong; see Garrett and Mitchell, 'Globalization, government spending, and taxation in the OECD', *European Journal of Political Research*, 39 (2001). Nita Rudra has shown that globalization has led to welfare state retrenchment in less developed countries – but also that strong labour power and democracy can offset this downward pressure; Rudra, 'Globalization and the decline of the welfare state in less-developed countries', *International Organization* 56 (2002). In sum, the available evidence is mixed and to some extent still ambiguous.

8   Jason Alexander, 'Power politics (a survey of the world economy)', *The Economist*, 7 Oct. 1995, p. 44, quoted in Jan Zielonka, *Explaining Europaralysis* (Basingstoke and London: Macmillan, 1998), p. 173.

9 Held, *Democracy and the Global Order*; Daniele Archibugi (ed.), *Debating Cosmopolitics* (London: Verso, 2003).
10 John Rawls, *A Theory of Justice* (Cambridge, Mass.: Harvard University Press, 1971).
11 Philippe Van Parijs, *Real Freedom for All: What (If Anything) Can Justify Capitalism?* (Oxford: Oxford University Press, 1995), p. 227.
12 Clearly this development is not problematic for many conservatives, for whom equality and justice are conflicting goals anyway, independently from the level of transnational economic flows.
13 Robert O. Keohane and Joseph S. Nye Jr, 'Introduction', in Joseph S. Nye Jr and John D. Donahue (eds), *Governance in a Globalizing World* (Washington DC: Brookings Institution Press, 2001).
14 Economic globalization is a complex phenomenon and one can well have a different opinion on each of its aspects. For instance, Jagdish Bhagwati is a leading advocate of free trade but at the same time strongly supports tighter controls on international capital flows; see Bhagwati, 'The capital myth', *Foreign Affairs*, 77 (1998). Thus the labels 'sceptic', 'deregulator', 'reverser' and 'internationalist' may refer to the specific issue under consideration (e.g. trade, short-term capital flows, foreign direct investment) and not necessarily to a person's attitude towards globalization in general.

1

The Disturbing Rise in Poverty and Inequality: Is It All a 'Big Lie'?

Robert Hunter Wade

The liberal argument says that world poverty and income inequality have both fallen over the past two decades or so for the first time in more than a century and a half.[1] This happy result is driven largely by the rising density of economic integration between countries ("globalization"). Therefore the current world "system" serves the great majority of the world's people well by most measures of well-being. Conversely, the anti-globalization movement and other peddlers of *fin de millénaire* doom have no serious empirical evidence to back up their claims. They are preaching, in the words of Martin Wolf of the *Financial Times*, "the big lie." Their favored policies would only cause more poverty and inequality.

Evidence from the current wave of globalization thus confirms the predictions of neoliberal economic theory – that more open economies are more prosperous, that as any one economy liberalizes it experiences a faster rate of progress, and that those who resist economic liberalization must be acting out of "special interests." The evidence also confirms the need for the WTO as the world's main agent for freeing up markets and harmonizing national regulations so that economic agents have a world "level playing field" undistorted by state restrictions.

In this chapter I summarize some doubts about the empirical evidence and causal relationships presented in support of the liberal claims. I then discuss a few of the deep structural causes at work in the world economy that may explain why the liberal argument is probably wrong.

Poverty

The World Bank is effectively the sole producer of the world poverty headcount. The Bank says, in the words of its president James Wolfensohn, that "Over the past 20 years the number of people living on less than $1 a day has fallen by 200 million, after rising steadily for 200 years."[2] The opening sentence of *World Development Indicators 2001* says, "Of the world's 6 billion people 1.2 billion live on less than $1 a day," the same number as in both 1987 and 1998.[3]

The count of people living in extreme poverty throughout the world inevitably has a large margin of error. But we can be reasonably confident that it is higher than the World Bank says, and that the trend has been rising over 1980–98, and especially 1987–98. I have space only to sketch a few of the reasons behind these conclusions.[4]

First, the comparison between 1980 and 1998 – 1.4 billion in extreme poverty in 1980, 1.2 billion in 1998 – is not legitimate because the Bank introduced a new methodology in the late 1990s, which makes the two figures non-comparable. The Bank has recalculated the poverty numbers with the new methodology only back to 1987, and we do not know what the 1980 figure would be if calculated in the same way as the later figure. The Bank's change of methodology amounts to (1) a change in the way the international poverty line was calculated from the official poverty lines of a sample of low- and middle-income countries; (2) a change in the international poverty line from $PPP1 per day to $PPP1.08 per day (PPP stands for purchasing power parity);[5] and (3) a change in the procedure for aggregating, country by country, the relative price changes between 1985 and 1993 (the dates of the two major

Table 1.1 Poverty rate 1993, using old and new World Bank methodology

	Old poverty rate (%)	New poverty rate (%)
Sub-Saharan Africa	39.1	49.7
Latin America	23.5	15.3
Middle East/N. Africa	4.1	1.9

The poverty rate is the proportion of the population living on less than $1 a day. The old rate is based on the 1985 PPP benchmark survey, the new rate is based on the one of 1993.
Source: Angus Deaton, "Counting the World's Poor: Problems and Possible Solutions," *World Bank Research Observer*, 16 (2001)

international price surveys for a standard bundle of goods and services).

Second, we do know, though, that the Bank's new methodology caused a huge change in the poverty count even for the same country in the same year using the same survey data.[6] Table 1.1 shows the methodology-induced changes by regions for 1993. Angus Deaton, who knows as much about poverty statistics as anyone, comments that "Changes of this size risk swamping real changes," "and it seems impossible to make statements about changes in world poverty when the ground underneath one's feet is changing in this way."[7]

Third, we also know that the new international poverty line of $PPP1.08 translates into *lower* national poverty lines in most countries. To be exact, it translates into lower national poverty lines in 77 percent of the 94 countries for which data are available, containing 82 percent of their population. The new international line lowers the old national line for China by 14 percent, for India by 9 percent, for the whole sample by an average of 13 percent.[8] It is likely that future "updating" of the international poverty line will continue to depress the true trend, because world-wide average consumption patterns (on which the international poverty line is based) are shifting toward services whose relative prices are much lower in poor than in rich countries, giving the false impression that the increase in the cost of the basic consumption goods required by the poor is lower than it is.

Fourth, the new methodology did not address a basic problem with the Bank's global (old or new) poverty line to do with *which* goods and services are included in the bundle against which relative purchasing power is being measured. The problem is that the Bank's line relates to a "general consumption" bundle, not to a basket of goods and services that makes sense for measuring poverty, such as food, clothing and shelter (though "$1 per day" does have intuitive appeal to a Western audience being asked to support aid). We have no way of knowing what proportion of food-clothing-shelter needs the Bank's poverty line captures. If the Bank used a basic needs poverty line rather than its present artificial one the number of absolute poor would probably rise, because the national poverty lines equivalent to a global basic needs poverty line expressed in US dollars would probably rise (maybe by as much as 25–50 percent). They would rise because the present PPP price indices include many services that are very cheap in developing countries (such as massages) but irrelevant to the poor – to the consumption bundle needed to avoid poverty – and therefore give a misleadingly high measure of the purchasing power of the incomes of the poor. Food and shelter are relatively expensive, and if they alone were included in the PPP exchange rate used to express the incomes of the poor in US dollars, national poverty lines would go up. Indeed, the rates of "extreme poverty" for Latin American countries using poverty lines based on calorific and demographic characteristics are roughly *twice* as high as those based on the World Bank's $1/day line.[9]

Fifth, the poverty headcount is very sensitive to the precise level of the global poverty line because income distribution in the vicinity of developing country poverty lines is typically fairly flat. Even a small increase in the line brings a large increase in the number of people below it. Hence we can expect that a shift to a poverty line

21

based on basic needs, which excludes services that are very cheap but irrelevant to the poor, would raise the number of people in extreme poverty by a significant amount.

Sixth, the Bank's poverty headcount comes from household surveys. Household surveys have a number of limitations that add up to a large margin of error in national poverty numbers and so also in the world totals. Some are well known, such as the exclusion of most of the benefits that people receive from publicly provided goods and services. Others are less well known, such as the sensitivity of the poverty headcount to the recall period used in the survey. The shorter the recall period the more expenditure is reported. India provides a striking example. A recent study suggests that a switch from the standard 30-day reporting period to a 7-day reporting period itself lifts 175 million people from poverty using the Indian official poverty line, a nearly 50 percent fall. Using the $1/day international line, which is higher, the fall would be even greater.[10]

Seventh, the PPP-adjusted income figures for China and India – the two most important countries for the overall trend – contain an even bigger component of guesswork than for most other significant countries. The main sources of purchasing power parity income figures (the Penn World Tables and the International Comparison Project) are based on two large-scale international price benchmarking exercises for calculating purchasing power parity exchange rates, one in 1985, the second in 1993, carried out in 60 countries in 1985, 110 countries in 1993. The government of China declined to participate in both. The purchasing power parity exchange rate for China is based on guestimates from small, ad hoc price surveys in a few cities, adjusted by rules of thumb to take account of the huge price differences between urban and rural areas and between eastern and western regions. The government of India declined to participate in the 1993 exercise. The price comparisons for India are extrapolations from 1985 qualified by small, ad hoc price surveys in later years. The lack of reliable price comparisons for China and India compromises any statement about trends in world poverty.[11]

In short, we should be cautious about accepting the World Bank's poverty headcount as even approximately correct. We do not know for sure whether the late 1990s revisions to the methodology and to the PPP numbers have the effect of raising or lowering the poverty headcount, and whether they alter the direction of the trend over the 1980s and 1990s. But it is likely that the Bank's numbers underestimate the true numbers, and the methodology applied at the end of the late 1990s makes the trend look better than it really is.

It is quite plausible that the *proportion* of the world's population living in extreme poverty (facing periods of food consumption too low to maintain health and well-being) has fallen over the past 20 years or so, thanks largely to fast economic growth in China and India. The broad trends in national data for these two countries, including life expectancy and other non-income measures, give grounds for confidence in this conclusion even allowing for large margins of error. Moreover the magnitude of world population increase over the past 20 years is so great that the Bank's poverty numbers would have to be *huge* underestimates for the proportion in extreme poverty not to have fallen. Any more precise statement about the absolute number of the world's people living in extreme poverty and the change in the number over time currently rests on quicksand.

Inequality

Many analysts claim that world income inequality fell sharply in the second half of the twentieth century, especially in the final quarter.[12] But in the past several years world income distribution has become a hot topic of debate in international economics and in sociology, and there is now even less agreement about income distribution than about poverty. Whereas we *could* get better data on the poor to the extent that the numbers would command general agreement, the issues in the measurement of inequality do not admit of best solutions.

The answer to the question "What is happening to world income inequality?" depends on choices among the following: (a) alternative measurements of income (GNP (gross national product) per capita converted to US dollars using market exchange rates or GNP per capita adjusted for differences in purchasing power across countries); (b) alternative samples of countries and alternative weightings of countries (each country weighted as one unit or by population); (c) alternative measures of distribution (the Gini or other average coefficient of inequality, or ratios of the income of the richer deciles of world population to that of poorer deciles, or average income of a set of developed countries to that of a set of developing countries); (d) national income accounts or household income and expenditure surveys. These choices make a big difference to the results, and there is no single best measure. Here are my abbreviated conclusions.[13]

Market exchange rates

If incomes of different countries are converted into a common numeraire (the US dollar) using market exchange rates the results are unambiguous. Whatever the other choices, world income distribution has become more unequal. No one disputes this. The dispute is about whether the figures mean anything. Most economists say that exchange rate based income measures are irrelevant, that GNP incomes should always be adjusted by purchasing power parity (PPP) exchange rates to take account of differences in purchasing power. The adjustment is made by using the same relative prices for all goods and services in all countries. Since the market prices of goods and services sold only locally (not internationally traded) are significantly cheaper in poor countries relative to the market prices of goods and services facing international competition, the adjustment generally raises the income of poor countries and lowers income of rich countries, making the distribution between them less unequal.

It is true that income comparisons based on market exchange rates suffer from distortions in official exchange rates and from sudden changes in the official exchange rate. Nevertheless, the argument that incomes converted via PPP exchange rates are always to be used in preference to incomes converted via market exchange rates should be rejected for conceptual and practical reasons. The practical reasons concern the intractable problems of knowing what the purchasing power parity figures mean, especially for China and India, and, before the early 1990s, for countries of the former Soviet Union. The conceptual reasons have to do with the fact that we may be interested in income and its distribution not only to measure relative total purchasing power (for which purpose PPP-adjusted income is a better proxy, *in principle*), but also to measure the relative purchasing power that residents of different countries have over goods and services produced in other countries. If we are interested in any of the questions about the economic and geopolitical impact of one country (or region) on the rest of the world – including the capacity of developing countries to repay their debts, to import capital goods, and to participate in or avoid marginalization in the international political economy – we should use market exchange rates. After all, the reason why many poor countries are hardly represented in negotiations that concern them directly is that they can't afford the cost of hotels, offices, and salaries in places like Washington DC and Geneva, which must be paid in hard currency bought at market exchange rates, not in PPP dollars. And the reason they cannot afford to pay the foreign exchange costs of living up to many of their international commitments – hiring foreign experts to help them exercise control over their banking sectors so that they can implement their part of the regime against money laundering, for example – likewise reflects their relatively low market-exchange-rate incomes. For all these reasons we need to pay attention to what is happening to market-exchange-rate world income distribution. It is widening fast.

Purchasing power parity

Purchasing power parity figures show trends in world income distribution that are more ambiguous than market exchange rate figures, more conditional on precisely which combination of measures one uses. But the evidence does strongly support the following three propositions.

1   If one uses decile measurements of inequality (richest decile of the world's population to median, poorest decile to median) rather than the Gini or other measure of inequality over the whole distribution, then PPP-adjusted income distribution has become *much more unequal* over the past two decades, whether countries are weighted equally or by population. World income *polarization*, in other words, has increased unambiguously.

2   If one uses a measurement of the entire distribution, and weights countries equally (China = Uganda), inequality between countries' average PPP-adjusted income has also *increased* since at least 1980. And if one measures inequality in terms of the dispersion of per capita GDPs across the world's (equally weighted) countries, this too *rose* between 1950 and 1998, and especially fast over the 1990s. The dispersion of per capita GDP (gross domestic product) growth rates has also risen over time, suggesting wider variation in performance among countries at each income level. One study using these dispersion measures concludes that there is "no doubt as to the existence of a definite trend towards distributive inequality worldwide, both across and within countries."[14]

3   If one uses a measurement of the entire distribution but weights countries by population, inequality between the country averages has been *constant or falling* since around 1980. This is the result that Martin Wolf, *The Economist*, and many others

26

celebrate. But it comes entirely from fast average growth in China and India. If they are excluded, even this measure of inequality shows inequality widening since 1980.

In any case this last measure – the average income of each country weighted by population – is interesting only as an approximation to what we are really interested in, which is income distribution among all the world's people or households regardless of which country they live in. We would not be interested in measuring income inequality within the United States by calculating the average income for each state and weighting it by their populations if we had data for all households.

One recent study makes an approximation to the distribution of income among all the world's people by combining between-country inequality in PPP-adjusted average incomes with within-country inequality. It finds that world inequality *widened* between 1980 and 1993 using all of four common measures of inequality over the entire distribution (and with countries weighted by population).[15]

Another recent study, based on the most comprehensive set of data drawn only from household income and expenditure surveys (it does not mix data from these surveys with data from national income accounts), finds a sharp *rise* in world inequality over as short a time as 1988 to 1993, using both the Gini coefficient and ratio (or polarization) measures (table 1.2).[16]

We have to be cautious about this finding partly because household surveys have the kinds of weaknesses described above (though these weaknesses do not make them worse than the alternative, national income accounts, which have their own problems), and partly because the five-year interval is very short, suggesting that some of the increase may be statistical noise.

In short, the only set of measurements where the evidence clearly supports the liberal argument of falling inequality is the one using *population-weighted countries' per capita PPP-adjusted incomes, plus a measure of inequality over the whole distribution, taking*

Table 1.2 World income distribution by households, 1988, 1993

	1988	*1993*	*% change*
Gini	0.63	0.67	+6
Richest decile/median	7.28	8.98	+23
Poorest decile/median	0.31	0.28	−10

Source: Data from Branko Milanovic, "True World Income Distribution, 1988 and 1993: First Calculations based on Household Surveys Alone," *Economic Journal*, 112 (Jan. 2002)

China's growth statistics at face value. On the other hand, the evidence of rising polarization (using decile ratios) is unambiguous, whatever the other choices of measures. And even measures of inequality over the whole distribution, when applied either to household survey data or to the combined inequality between countries and within countries (as distinct from only inequality between countries' average income), show a widening of inequality.

In short, we can say that world interpersonal income distribution has certainly become more unequal over the past two decades when measured in terms of market exchange rates. Measured in terms of purchasing power parity and *average* inequality (such as the Gini coefficient) it has *probably* either remained fairly constant or increased; it has almost certainly not decreased with globalization, as the liberal argument claims. Measured in terms of top to median and bottom to median, income polarization has *increased*, even using PPP-adjusted incomes. A rising proportion of the world's population is living at the ends of the world income distribution; and a rising share of the world's income is going to those at the top.[17]

Our measures of inequality refer to relative incomes, not absolute incomes. So inequality between developing countries as a group and developed countries as a group remains constant if the ratio of developing country income to developed country income remains at 5 percent. But this of course implies a big rise in the absolute size of the gap. In the general case the absolute gap between a country with average income of $1,000 growing at 6 percent and a country with average income of $30,000 growing at 1 percent continues to widen until after the fortieth year! China and India are reducing the absolute gap with the faltering middle-income states like Mexico, Brazil, Russia and Argentina, but they are not reducing the absolute gap between their average incomes and the averages of the countries of North America, Western Europe and Japan. In the world at large, absolute gaps are increasing fast and will continue to do so for several generations.

Should we be worried about rising income inequality and widening absolute gaps? Many people say that rising inequality, relative or absolute, should not be a concern – certainly not a target of public policy – provided the poor are not becoming worse off as a result of widening inequality. This applies within countries and even more so to inequalities between countries. The question of whether we should be concerned about rising inequalities between countries needs a good deal more research than it has received.

On the face of it, the more globalized the world becomes, the more the reasons why we might be concerned about within-country inequalities also apply to between-country inequalities. Educated people who earlier compared themselves to others in their neighborhood or nation now compare themselves to others in much richer nations, and feel relatively deprived. In this way the high and rising (relative and absolute) gap in incomes of the richest countries and the poorer ones is bound to affect national political economy in the poorer states. It may, for example, predispose the elites to be more corrupt as they compare themselves to elites in rich countries and squeeze their own populations in order to sustain a comparable living standard. It may encourage the educated people of poor countries to migrate to the rich countries, and encourage unskilled people to seek illegal entry. It may generate conflict between states, and – because the market-exchange-rate income gap is so big – make it cheap for rich states to intervene to support one side or the other in civil strife. These effects may be presumed to operate even if relative income gaps are declining but absolute income gaps are widening.

Globalization

What is the evidence that globalization – rising integration of poorer countries into the world economy, as seen in rising trade/GDP, foreign direct investment/GDP, and the like – is the world's most powerful means of reducing poverty and inequality?

Clearly the proposition is not well supported at the world level if we agree that globalization has been rising while income inequality and poverty have not been falling. But it might still be possible to argue that globalization explains differences between countries: that more globalized countries have a better record of economic growth, poverty reduction and inequality reduction than less globalized ones.

This is what World Bank studies claim. One of the best known, *Globalization, Growth and Poverty*,[18] distinguishes "newly globalizing" or "more globalized" countries from "nonglobalizing" or "less globalized" countries. It measures globalizing by *changes* in the ratio of trade to GDP between 1977 and 1997. Ranking developing countries by the change, it calls the top third the globalizing or more globalized countries, and the remaining two-thirds are called less globalized countries or weak globalizers. The globalizing countries are then found to have had faster economic growth, no increase in inequality, and faster reduction of poverty than the weak globalizers. "Thus, globalization clearly can be a force for poverty reduction."

The argument is undermined by the use of "change in trade/GDP" as the measure of globalization.[19] The list of "globalizers" includes China and India, as well as countries like Nepal, Côte d'Ivoire, Rwanda, Haiti, and Argentina. As the cases of China and India suggest, it is quite possible that "more globalized" countries are less open in terms of *levels* of integration than "less globalized" countries; and also less open in terms of trade policy than "less globalized" countries. A country with very high trade/GDP and very free trade could still be categorized as a weak globalizer. It turns out that the globalizing countries are mainly ones that initially had very *low* trade/GDP in 1977. Many of them still had relatively low trade/GDP at the *end* of the period, in 1997 – and this does not just reflect the fact that larger economies tend to have lower ratios of trade/GDP. To call them globalizers, and countries with much higher ratios of trade/GDP nonglobalizers, is an audacious use of language.

Excluding countries with high but not rising levels of trade to GDP from the category of more globalized excludes many very poor countries dependent on a few natural resource commodity exports, which have had very poor economic growth. The structure of their economy and the low skill endowment of the population make them very dependent on trade. If they were included as globalized their poor economic performance would cast doubt on the proposition that the more globalized countries have the best performance.

The inclusion of China and India as globalizers – with their good economic performance over the past one or two decades attributed in large part to their globalization – guarantees that the globalized will show better performance than the nonglobalized. But two big facts question the Bank's argument. First, China and India experienced a sharp increase in the trend rate of growth about a decade prior to their liberalizing trade and investment reforms. Second, they have achieved their relatively fast rise in trade/GDP with policies far from the liberal trade and investment policies advocated by the globalists. They remain highly protected economies. The World Bank would be the first to denounce their current trade policies and internal market-restricting policies as inhibiting to growth and efficiency if they had not been growing fast.

Their experience – and that of Japan, South Korea and Taiwan earlier – shows that countries do not have to adopt liberal trade policies in order to reap benefits from trade, to grow fast, and to grow an industrial structure able to produce an increasing proportion of national consumption.[20] They all experienced relatively fast growth behind protective barriers, and fast growth fueled rapid trade expansion increasingly focused on capital goods and intermediate goods. As they became richer they tended to liberalize their trade – providing the basis for the common misunderstanding that trade liberalization fueled their growth. For all the Bank study's qualifications (such as "We label the top third 'more globalized' [that is, bigger increase in trade/GDP] without in any sense implying that they adopted pro-trade policies. The rise in trade may have been due to other policies or even to pure chance"), it concludes that trade liberalization has been the driving force of the increase in developing countries' trade. "The result of this trade liberalization in the developing world has been a large increase in both imports and exports." On this questionable proposition the Bank rests its case for trade liberalization as a central element in its core development recipe for all countries.

The Bank's argument about the benign effects of globalization on growth, poverty and income distribution does not survive scrutiny. The argument is also questioned by a recent cross-country study of the relationship between openness and income equality. This study finds that among the subset of countries with low and middle levels of average income (below roughly $5,000 per capita in purchasing power terms, or below that of Chile and the Czech Republic), higher levels of trade openness are associated with *more* inequality, while among higher-income countries more openness goes with more equality.[21]

Why is globalization probably not reducing poverty and inequality?

If the number of people in absolute poverty is probably not falling and probably higher than the World Bank says, and if income inequality by several plausible measures (especially those that measure polarization) is not falling and probably rising, why? Not because of the failure of industrialization in developing countries. If we take the share of GDP in manufacturing in developing countries as a group and developed countries as a group, we find a remarkable convergence – developing countries now have a *bigger* share of GDP in manufacturing than developed. But each additional increment of manufacturing in developing countries is yielding less income over time. This is quite contrary to the understandings of the "modernization" champions of the 1950s to 1980s, ancestors of today's globalists. They thought that (market-friendly) industrialization would be the vehicle to carry developing countries to the living standards of the developed world. The failure of this prediction may help to explain why industrialization as such is given little attention in today's development agenda. It has virtually disappeared from the concerns of the World Bank, which has switched its notion of development from production and economic growth to human needs and capabilities.

If failure to industrialize is not the culprit, what other factors might explain widening inequality? What is causing a shift in the distribution of world population toward the extremes of the world income distribution and a shift in the distribution of world income toward the top end of the distribution? At the bottom end, population is growing several times faster in the low-income zone than in the rich zone, raising the share of world population living in countries in the low-income zone. Also at the bottom end, the terms of trade facing developing countries – the prices of their exports, especially primary commodities, over the prices of their imports from developed countries – have fallen sharply over the past two decades, depressing the share of world income going to the low-income zone.[22] The harnessing of China's vast reservoirs of labor has particularly depressed the terms of trade for developing country manufactures.

Regional, not global, focus of multinational corporations

At the top end, we see that – contrary to the common idea of markets and firms becoming increasingly global – most of the Fortune 500 biggest multinational corporations depend for most of their sales on their home region, whether North America, the European Union, or East Asia (the "Triad").[23] Less than a dozen are "global" in their sales, even in the restricted sense of having 20 percent or more of total sales (from parents and subsidiaries) in each of these three regions. They sell a negligible proportion of total sales in developing countries outside of East Asia. Moreover, their focus on just one of the three Triad regions intensified in the second half of the 1990s as compared with the first half. The foreign operations of the multinationals became less profitable than their home-based operations in the second half of the 1990s, having been more profitable in the first half of the 1990s. Multinational corporations are "regionalizing," not "globalizing."

Spatial clustering of high value-added activities

Underlying the observed patterns of location, trade and prices is a general property of modern economic growth related to spatial clustering. We know that some kinds of economic activities and production methods are more lucrative than others, have stronger unpriced spillover benefits, and more positive effects on growth and productivity; and that countries and regions with higher proportions of such activities enjoy higher levels of real incomes. We also know that in free market conditions (not as a result of market "imperfections") the high value-added activities – in manufacturing and in services – cluster in the high-cost, high-wage zone of the world economy. German skilled workers cost about 15 times as much to employ as Chinese skilled workers; yet Germany remains a powerful center of manufacturing.

When it comes to the higher value-added activities, in other words, locations are "sticky," for several reasons. First, costs per unit of output, especially labor costs, may not be lower in the lower wage zone, because lower wages may be more than offset by lower productivity. In any case, the cost of employing people has fallen to a small proportion of total costs in automated assembly operations, often 10 percent or less. As the technology content of many engineering products, including vehicle parts and aircraft, becomes increasingly sophisticated, this raises the premium on the company keeping highly skilled workers to develop and manufacture these products – by paying them highly.

Second, many forms of higher value-added activities are subject both to increasing returns to scale and to linkage or network effects (which lower transactions costs for firms located in physical or social proximity). In the presence of increasing returns to scale and linkages much of the liberal argument about the virtues of private property, competition and specialization based on comparative advantage in spreading the benefits of economic growth "evenly" loses force. On the contrary, we expect tendencies towards divergence, polarization, twin peaks.[24]

Increasing returns and network effects may show up inside firms. The "capability" of a firm relative to that of rivals (the maximum quality level it can achieve, and its cost of production) depends not only on the sum of the skills of its workforce, but also on the *collective* or firm-level knowledge and social organization of its employees; and much of this knowledge and social organization is essentially *tacit*, transferred mainly through face-to-face relationships – not able to be transferred easily from place to place in the form of (technical and organizational) blueprints or embodied in machinery.[25] If a firm were to move to a lower wage zone and some of its employees were not mobile, the costs to the firm's capacity, including the loss of tacit knowledge, might outweigh the advantages of relocation.

Manufacturing firms in the OECD countries are engaged in dense input–output linkages with other firms. (About two-thirds of manufacturing output in the OECD is sold by one firm to another firm.) The presence of a dense and spatially concentrated network of input–output linkages provides spillover benefits to firms in the network. So does the presence of well-functioning factor markets and a supply of formally educated people able to gain technology-specific (and partly tacit) knowledge at low cost. And as noted, tacit knowledge, whose economic value typically increases even as the ratio of tacit to codified knowledge falls with computerization, is transferred more easily within networks underpinned by social relationships, cultural similarity, and the disposition to trust. These network effects compound the tendency for any one firm not to move to a low-wage zone, or to move only its *low* value-added, assembly activities by outsourcing or establishing subsidiaries while keeping other activities that depend on varied inputs, tacit knowledge and social contacts in the core.

All the more so because for many products and services, quality and value added go up not continuously but in steps. (Ballbearings below a quality threshold are useless.) Getting to higher steps may require big investments, critical masses, targeted assistance from public entities, and long-term supply contracts with multinational corporations seeking local suppliers. "Normal" market processes can keep producers and countries stuck at low steps.

In some of the biggest manufacturing sectors – including electronics and vehicles – parent companies based in the high-income zone have formed increasingly concentrated vertical production networks through which they obtain the major share of value added by their control of proprietary technology, branding and marketing. They have put an increasing proportion of routine manufacturing operations in lower tier suppliers in the low-income zone, often locally owned companies; and then used their market power and intense competition among the lower tier suppliers to extract more value added from them. When global recession comes the lower tier suppliers are first to suffer, especially those locked into Japanese production hierarchies.

This is not the end of the story. At the next round the greater wealth and variety of economic activities in the high-wage zone –

not to mention fiscal redistribution, a legal system that supports limited liability, and a socially more homogeneous population – mean that it can more readily absorb the Schumpeterian shocks from innovation and bankruptcies, as activity shifts from products and processes with more intense competition to those with less competition closer to the innovation end. There is less resistance to the "creative destruction" of market processes, even though organizing people to pursue common objectives, including resistance, tends to be easier than in the low-wage zone. Enron may go bankrupt but there are plenty more companies to take on its business and employ its employees.

These effects – plus limited labor movement from the low-wage zone to the high-wage zone when international borders intervene – help to explain a stably "divided world" in which high wages remain high in one zone while low wages elsewhere stay low, even as the industrialization gap has been eliminated. The important point is that well-functioning free markets in a highly economically interdependent or globalized world produce, "spontaneously," a stable equilibrium division of activities between the high-wage zone and the low-wage zone – one that is hardly desirable for the low-wage zone. Or to connect the argument to the empirical findings on openness and inequality reported earlier, one might hypothesize that in low-income developing countries higher levels of trade to GDP raise the income share of the rich, who have education and control over critical trade-related services, while shrinking the share of the bulk of the population with minimal or no education; and the consumption preferences of the rich lock the low-income countries into dependence on imports of consumption goods from the high-income countries, restricting the replacement of imports by local production that is the key to expanding prosperity. Oligopolistic industrial organization in the high-income zone reinforces the inequalities by supporting mark-up pricing, and prompting declining terms of trade for the low-wage zone.

Even about East Asia we should not get too optimistic. Only a minuscule portion of world R&D work is done in (non-Japan)

East Asia; virtually all of it continues to be done in the developed countries of North America, Western Europe and Japan. Even Singapore, that looks to be an Asian center of research and development, does not do "real" R&D; its R&D labs mostly concentrate on adapting products developed in North America and Europe for the regional market and listening in on what competitors are doing.[26] So much for the much heralded "globalization of R&D." China still relies heavily on foreign investment for its higher tech manufactured output; and foreign investment is still mainly seeking low-cost labor, tax breaks and implied promises of protection, as distinct from rapidly rising skills. Its export competitiveness remains concentrated in labor-intensive products of foreign-owned factories. Even its information technology engineering complex around Shanghai depends heavily on Taiwanese and other foreign know-how. Japanese alarm bells have been ringing at graphs showing Japan's personal computer exports to the US falling as China's rise; but the figures conceal the fact that the computers are assembled in China using high value-added technology from Japan and elsewhere. Some of the technology is spilling into the heads of the millions of Chinese employees, almost certainly more than is occurring in other developing countries. But added to doubts about the accuracy of China's growth statistics, these qualifications should caution us about a scenario of declining world income inequality that rests on China's continued fast growth and transformation.

In short, the benign effects of free markets in spreading benefits around the world, as celebrated in the liberal argument, may be offset by tendencies toward increasing returns and spatially concentrated networks, seen in the agglomeration of high value-added activities in the high-income zone. These tendencies can maintain a stable division between a high value-added, high-wage zone and a low value-added, low-wage zone – even as ratios of manufacturing to GDP, total trade/GDP, and manufacturing exports/total exports rise in the latter.

There are other basic drivers as well. They include the transformations of capitalism from assembly lines to information manipulation, from manufacturing to finance, that place higher premiums on skills and education and penalize those without. They include the international monetary system in place since the breakdown of the Bretton Woods system in the early 1970s, which among other things put pressure on the more successful developing countries – those that have liberalized their capital account – to limit their growth rates so as to limit the risk of crisis triggered by sudden capital flight. And the drivers include the withdrawal of support by international financial institutions such as the World Bank and the International Monetary Fund for industrial policies aimed at creating import-replacing industries and ones that might challenge those of the West. What is clear is that open, well-functioning markets need not produce convergence between parts of the low-income zone and the high-income zone, and can produce divergence, polarization; which underlines the need for nonmarket measures of intervention if sizable fractions of the world's population are to catch up in living standards over the next half century or so.

Conclusions

The globalists set up a Manichean dichotomy between pro-globalist and anti-globalist positions. My conclusions constitute a third way. I agree with the globalizers that economic growth is essential to raise the living standards of the world's poorer people (as are changes in our measures of economic growth to weigh environmental quality and public services properly). I agree that more open markets in the West for labor-intensive and land-intensive exports from developing countries would help, and that more foreign direct investment from the West, more technology transfer, is generally to be welcomed. Attempts at national self-sufficiency are foolish, though few countries apart from North Korea are trying and nobody is claiming that China would be better off if it had remained as closed as before 1978. Protectionist business associations and trade unions in the wealthiest countries, who claim that any threat to jobs must be because of "unfair competition" from elsewhere, are generally to be resisted.

I part company from the globalists in my reading of the trends in poverty and income distribution. On poverty I say that we must be agnostic, because our current statistics are too deficient to yield a confident answer (though it is quite plausible that the *proportion* of the world's population in extreme poverty has fallen in the past two decades). My weaker conclusion is that the numbers are probably higher than the World Bank says, and have probably been rising over the past two decades. On income distribution I say that world inequality is increasing when incomes are measured in current exchange rates (and this is more relevant than PPP incomes for judging the relative impacts of one part of the world on others, including the participation or marginalization of developing countries in international rule-making fora, and the ability to borrow and repay loans). Income inequality is increasing too when PPP-adjusted inequality is measured in terms of ratios of richer to poorer, which better captures the idea of polarization. All the several other combinations of measures yield more ambiguous trend results, more contingent on things like the time period and the countries included in the sample. But several recent independent studies, using different methodologies, different samples, different time periods, do find that world income inequality has risen since the early 1980s. It is simply disingenuous to keep repeating that world income distribution has become more equal as undeniable fact. Taken as a whole the evidence allows no such confidence.

Finally, absolute income gaps between the West and the rest are widening, even in the case of countries growing relatively fast like China and India, and are likely to go on widening for another half century at least. No one disputes this, but globalists tend to focus on relative incomes only. I suggested several kinds of negative effects likely to follow from widening absolute income gaps even when relative income gaps are falling.

I also part company with the globalists by giving higher priority to reductions not only in world poverty but also in world income inequality. This cannot be a direct objective of public policy, which has to focus on inequalities within nation-states or (via trade rules, aid, etc.) inequalities among states. But it can be taken as a higher level objective and built into our measures of world development. We should not accept the commonly heard assertion that widening world income inequality is not a negative provided that "real" indicators like life expectancy are improving and the proportion living in extreme poverty is going down.

I disagree with the globalist proposition that globalization is the driver of the allegedly positive poverty and inequality results. The point is not that "globalization" cannot be precisely defined for these purposes; it is that the definitions used in the globalists' studies do not stand scrutiny. In particular, the main World Bank studies, by defining globalization in terms of *increases* in trade/GDP or foreign direct investment/GDP and ignoring the level, manage to include China and India as "globalizers" or "open economies" and many highly open, trade-dependent, badly performing African countries as "nonglobalizers." Having constructed a definition of a globalized country that puts China and India into this category, the Bank does not go on to emphasize that the economic policies of the best-performing "globalizers" – China in particular – are far from the core economic policy package that it has recommended over the past two decades.

At the very least, analysts have to separate out the effect of country size on trade/GDP levels from other factors determining trade/GDP, including trade policies; and make a clear distinction between statements about (1) levels of trade, (2) changes in levels, (3) restrictiveness or openness of trade policy, and (4) changes in restrictiveness of policy. These distinctions are fudged in common globalist assertions that "openness is a necessary – though not sufficient – part of modern economic growth," or assertions that the World Bank studies referred to earlier demonstrate that "more open" economies perform better than "less open."

If global inequality is widening by plausible measures and the number of people in extreme poverty probably not falling, we cannot conclude that globalization – or the spread of free-market relations – is moving the world in the right direction, with Africa's poverty as a special case in need of international attention. The balance of probability is that – like global warming – the world is moving in the wrong direction in terms of poverty and income inequality, which strengthens the case for applying the precautionary principle and revisiting development prescriptions and the design of the international economic regime.

We need to reintroduce a distinction that has dropped out of the development lexicon, between "external" integration and "internal" integration. "Integration" in today's development discourse refers to integration of a national economy into world markets, or external integration, and it is taken for granted that more external integration will automatically stimulate more internal integration between sectors (rural–urban, consumer goods–intermediate goods, etc.) and between wages, consumption, and production. On the contrary, much evidence suggests that internal integration – especially by replacing current imports with national production and thereby generating demands for new kinds of imports – needs to be stimulated by state-led industrial policy, and that higher internal integration can propel higher external integration.[27]

We also need to revisit the mandate and procedures of the multilateral economic organizations, which all – the WTO especially – assume that more market access is always better and that differences in market regulations between national markets are an undesirable obstacle to trade. The question is how to reconfigure them so as to legitimize more privileges for developing countries and eliminate requirements for "reciprocity," "national treatment" and "best practice" international standards. If globalization as presently structured were working to reduce poverty and inequality on a world scale this would not be necessary. As I have shown here, it is probably not, and we in the rich world will eventually suffer the consequences.

Notes

I thank Sanjay Reddy, Michael Ward, Branko Milanovic, Ron Dore, Martin Wolf, and James Galbraith for good discussions; and the Crisis States Program, DESTIN, London School of Economics, for financial support. See further my essays, "Winners and Losers: The Global Distribution of Income is Becoming More Unequal; That Should be a Matter of Greater Concern Than It Is," By Invitation, *The Economist*, Apr. 28, 2001, pp. 79–81, republished in *Globalisation* (London: The Economist, 2001); "The Rising Inequality of World Income Distribution," *Finance and Development*, 38, no. 4 (Dec. 2001); "Prospect Debate: Are Global Poverty and Inequality Getting Worse?" *Prospect*, Mar. 2002, pp. 16–21.

1 In the words of Martin Wolf, "Evidence suggests the 1980s and 1990s were decades of declining global inequality and reductions in the proportion of the world's population in extreme poverty"; "Doing More Harm than Good," *Financial Times*, May 8, 2002. See also Wolf, "A Stepping Stone from Poverty," *Financial Times*, Dec. 19, 2001, and "The Big Lie of Global Inequality," Feb. 8, 2000.

2 World Bank, *World Development Indicators 2002*, Foreword (Washington DC: World Bank, 2002). Also, World Bank, *Global Economic Prospects and the Developing Countries 2002: Making Trade Work for the World's Poor* (Washington DC: World Bank, 2002), p. 30.

3 World Bank, *World Development Indicators 2001* (Washington DC: World Bank, 2001), p. 3. The $1 a day is measured in purchasing power parity; see note 5 below. See also *Globalization, Growth, and Poverty: Building an Inclusive World Economy* (Oxford: World Bank and Oxford University Press, 2002); Angus Deaton, "Is World Poverty Falling?" *Finance and Development*, forthcoming.

4 I am indebted to Sanjay Reddy for discussions about the Bank's methodology. See his paper with Thomas Pogge, "How Not to Count the Poor," June 2002, at www.socialanalysis.org. Also, Massoud Karshenas, "Measurement and Nature of Absolute Poverty in Least Developed Countries," typescript, Economics Department, School for Oriental and African Studies, University of London, Jan. 2002.

5 Purchasing power parity is a method of adjusting relative incomes in different countries to take account of the fact that market exchange

43

rates do not accurately reflect purchasing power – as in the common observation that poor Americans feel rich in India and rich Indians feel poor in the US.

6 The new results were published in World Bank, *World Development Report 2000/01* (Washington DC: World Bank, 2000).

7 Angus Deaton, "Counting the World's Poor: Problems and Possible Solutions," *World Bank Research Observer*, 16 (2001), pp. 125–47, at p. 128.

8 Reddy and Pogge, "How Not to Count the Poor."

9 For example, Brazil's extreme poverty rate according to the line established by the Comisión Económica para América Latina y el Caribe (CEPAL) was 14%, and according to the World Bank for roughly the same recent year, 5%; Bolivia, 23%, and 11%; Chile, 8%, and 4%; Colombia, 24%, and 11%; Mexico, 21%, and 18%: *Panorama Social de America Latina 2000–01*, CEPAL, Sept. 2001, p. 51.

10 Reported in Deaton, "Counting the World's Poor."

11 See Reddy and Pogge, "How Not to Count the Poor."

12 For example, Paul Ormerod, "Inequality: The Long View," *Prospect*, Aug./Sept. 2000. See also Robert Wright, "Global Happiness," *Prospect*, Dec. 2000. They both make the same strong statement about world income distribution: it has become more equal at the same time as globalization has accelerated. Martin Wolf of the *Financial Times* champions the idea that globalization improves global income distribution. See, for example, "Growth Makes the Poor Richer," *Financial Times*, Jan. 24, 2001: "reversing the effects of globalization might increase equality as the critics claim, but it would be an equality of destitution." Ian Castles, former Australian Statistician, claims that "most studies suggest that the past 25 years have seen a reversal in the trend towards widening global inequalities which had been proceeding for two centuries" (letter to *The Economist*, May 26, 2001).

13 In addition to the studies referenced elsewhere I draw on Glen Firebaugh, "Empirics of World Income Inequality," *American Journal of Sociology*, 104 (1999); C. Jones, "On the Evolution of World Income Distribution," *Journal of Economic Perspectives*, 11 (1997); Lant Pritchett, "Divergence: Big Time," *Journal of Economic Perspectives*, 11 (1997); Danny Quah, "Empirics for Growth and Distribution: Stratification, Polarization, and Convergence Clubs,"

Journal of Economic Growth, 2 (1997); United Nations Development Program, *Human Development Report 1999* (New York: UNDP, 1999); Ravi Kanbur, "Conceptual Challenges in Poverty and Inequality: One Development Economist's Perspective," WP2002–09, Dept of Applied Economics, Cornell University, Apr. 2002; Roberto Korzeniewicz and Timothy Moran, "World-Economic Trends in the Distribution of Income, 1965–1992," *American Journal of Sociology*, 102 (1997), pp. 1000–39; Roberto Korzeniewicz and Timothy Moran, "Measuring World Income Inequalities," *American Journal of Sociology*, 106 (2000), pp. 209–14.

14   *Globalization and Development*, Economic Commission for Latin America and the Caribbean (ECLAC), Apr. 2002, p. 85. The dispersion of per capita GDP/PPP is measured as the average logarithmic deviation, the dispersion of growth rates as the standard deviation.

15   Steve Dowrick and Muhammad Akmal, "Explaining Contradictory Trends in Global Income Inequality: A Tale of Two Biasses," Faculty of Economics and Commerce, Australian National University, 29 Mar., 2001, available on http://ecocomm.anu.edu.au/economics/staff/dowrick/dowrick.html. They find that world inequality increased between 1980 and 1993 using Gini, Theil, coefficient of variation, and the variance of log income.

16   Branko Milanovic, "True World Income Distribution, 1988 and 1993: First Calculations based on Household Surveys Alone," *Economic Journal*, 112 (Jan. 2002), pp. 51–92. Milanovic is currently working on 1998 data.

17   More doubts are cast on the falling inequality hypothesis by trends in industrial pay inequality within countries. Pay inequality within countries was stable or declining from the early 1960s to 1982, then sharply increased from 1982 to the present. The year 1982 marks a dramatic turning point toward greater inequality in industrial pay worldwide. See the work of James Galbraith and collaborators in the University of Texas Inequality Project, http://utip.gov.utexas.edu.

18   *Globalization, Growth, and Poverty: Building an Inclusive World Economy*, World Bank Policy Research Report (Oxford: World Bank and Oxford University Press, 2002).

19   In this section I draw on the arguments of Dani Rodrik, *The New Global Economy and the Developing Countries: Making Openness Work*, Overseas Development Council (Washington DC: Johns

Hopkins University Press, 1999); "Trading in Illusions," *Foreign Policy*, 123 (Mar./Apr. 2001).

20 Robert Wade, *Governing the Market* (Princeton: Princeton University Press, 1990).

21 Branko Milanovic, "Can We Discern the Effect of Globalization on Income Distribution? Evidence from Household Budget Surveys," World Bank Policy Research Working Paper 2876, Apr. 2002, at http://econ.worldbank.org. Milanovic finds that in countries below the average income of about $PPP5,000 higher levels of openness (imports plus exports/GDP) are associated with lower income shares of the bottom 80 percent of the population.

22 *Globalization and Development*, Box 2.1, p. 38.

23 Michael Gestrin, Rory Knight and Alan M. Rugman, "The Templeton Global Performance Index," Templeton College, University of Oxford, 1999, 2000 and 2001, at www.templeton.ox.ac.uk.

24 This is the non-neoclassical realm of analysts such as Alfred Marshall, Allyn A. Young, Nicholas Kaldor, Gunnar Myrdal, Albert Hirschman, Arthur Lewis, Paul Krugman, and Jane Jacobs; and also Karl Marx, whose defining features of capitalism included "the centralization of capital" and "the entanglement of all peoples in the net of the world-market."

25 I draw on John Sutton, "Rich Trades, Scarce Capabilities: Industrial Development Revisited," Keynes Lecture, British Academy, Oct. 2000. Also, Ralph Gomory and William Baumol, "Toward a Theory of Industrial Policy-Retainable Industries," C. V. Starr Center for Applied Economics, New York University, RR 92–54, Dec. 1992; Michael Porter, "Clusters and the New Economics of Competition," *Harvard Business Review*, 76, no. 6 (1998), pp. 77–90; Masahisa Fujita, Paul Krugman, and Anthony Venables, *The Spatial Economy: Cities, Regions, and International Trade* (Cambridge, Mass.: MIT Press, 1999).

26 Alice H. Amsden, Ted Tschang and Akira Goto, "A New Classification of R&D Characteristics for International Comparison (with a Singapore Case Study)," Asian Development Bank Institute, Tokyo, Dec. 2001.

27 Wade, *Governing the Market*. Also, Jane Jacobs, *Cities and the Wealth of Nations: Principles of Economic Life* (New York: Random House, 1984).

2

Globalization and Development

Joseph E. Stiglitz

The issue of development is one of the most important facing the world today. With approximately 20 percent of the world's population living on less than $1 a day, 50 percent on less than $2 a day, the challenges are enormous.[1] In the last century, we have seen that development is possible. What has been accomplished, for instance, in the countries of East Asia is much more than anybody anticipated or perhaps even hoped for 50 years ago. Incomes in a country like South Korea have increased more than eight-fold. Forty years ago the incomes per capita of India and Korea were roughly comparable; today Korea's is eight times that of India.

While development is clearly possible, it is far from inevitable. In fact in parts of the world and most notably in Africa, incomes have steadily declined since independence from colonial rule. There have been exceptions. There has been steady growth in a few countries, for instance in a small country like Botswana, but those cases are a rarity, and even Botswana's success is being called into question by the spread of AIDS.

Recent developments in Latin America are instructive. The optimism that was quite prevalent in Latin America at the beginning of the last decade and through the middle of the 1990s has now been shattered. The early 1990s saw relatively rapid growth in most of the countries of Latin America. There were democratic reforms and there were also marked changes in economic policy. But, beginning in 1995 with the crisis in Mexico, the so-called Tequila crisis, and then even more so with the global economic crisis in 1997, country after country faced recession, stagnation, or worse.

The most recent example is Argentina. The question that is being debated in much of Latin America is whether reform has failed Latin America or globalization has failed Latin America? In some sense, though, those two issues are really the same, because a key part of the reform agenda was globalization. As people have begun to look at these experiences more closely, a new view of the whole reform movement that characterized the early 1990s has emerged.

The rapid growth of that first half of the decade can be seen today as little more than a partial catch-up of the lost decade of the 1980s, which was itself a consequence of the mismanagement of the debt crisis by the IMF at the beginning of the 1980s. Not only was the growth that occurred in the early 1990s little more than a catch-up, but it also appears to have been unsustainable. It exposed countries to enormous risks, to which they were not capable of adapting. Argentina, the most recent failure, was for a long time the poster-child of the IMF and the Washington consensus policies that it pushed. Experience has shown that the IMF is a fair-weather friend: it will stick by you when things are going well, but when things look bad, all kinds of criticisms are advanced: what you did was incomplete, insufficient, the crisis was your own fault and you deserved it!

How to mismanage economic crises

In the summer of 2001, the IMF gave Argentina an $8 billion loan, which is not a modest sum. We work very hard to tell countries they have to spend their money well, but if you look at the amount that has been squandered in the misguided attempts to maintain overvalued exchange rates in Argentina, Brazil, or Russia, we are talking about magnitudes that amount to $10 billion or $50 billion – amounts that look small compared to that put on the table in East Asia. At a snap of a finger the IMF can throw away $50 billion, but then criticize countries for misspending $100,000 or $1 million. This reminds me of the expression "penny wise, pound foolish." Argentina represents only the latest case, and the experience there actually is telling.

We have to put these large bailouts in perspective. Conventional rhetoric has it that it is the taxpayers in the US, in the UK, etc., who are putting up the money. This is wrong. The money is almost always repaid. It comes out of the pockets of the taxpayers in the countries affected. So, when the IMF in 1998 lent Russia $6 billion and that money the next day wound up in Cypriot and Swiss bank accounts, it was not the money from the IMF or the United States that really was lost: it is Russian taxpayers who will have to repay that money. It is not a gift; it is a loan – and that loan will be repaid. You can always be more generous with the money of other countries.

In the case of Argentina, the Bush/O'Neill Administration has railed against the big bailouts that characterized the Clinton Administration, and I think quite rightly. But when it came to Argentina, they were willing to try once more. At least some of the executive directors (the board of the IMF that must approve all loans) knew that it would not work. One of them said to me, "Well, it's a going away present for Stan Fisher [the first deputy managing director of the IMF who was about to depart the Fund] – an $8 billion present," a perspective that then was confirmed by at least one other executive director. The phenomenon, of throwing good money after bad, while long derided by economists (who emphasize that bygones are bygones), has been frequently observed by scholars of organizations, who refer to it as *escalating commitment*. It is hard to admit mistakes, especially when the costs of continuing in the mistaken direction are borne by others.

Even at the time, it was clear that the probability that the bailout would work was extremely low. The Argentinian peso was badly overvalued, and while at the *official* exchange rate the debt was manageable, so long as the interest rates remained reasonable, at a more reasonable exchange rate the debt/GDP ratio was quite high, and markets, recognizing the high probability of a devaluation and a default (they were right), insisted on compensatingly high interest rates. The only circumstance in which it might have worked was a crash of the US dollar: being linked to the dollar, Argentina's currency would be devalued and Argentina would have been able to export a little bit more. Maybe somebody was praying for a fall of the dollar, but it is unlikely that even that would have worked, since then Argentina would have been hurt by the resulting global turmoil. In any case the failure of the IMF bailout in Argentina (as elsewhere) was predictable and predicted. In the meanwhile the $8 billion did what this kind of money has done in country after country: the money went to maintain free convertibility of the Argentinian peso to the dollar, on a one-to-one basis, for a little bit longer. (The *market* equilibrium – or at least the exchange rate that prevailed after the crash – was markedly lower, at more than 3 pesos to the dollar.) The loan thus allowed a few more Argentinians to get their money out, a few more American and other Western banks to get repaid before the crash, but the overall consequences for Argentina were all the worse, because as it went into default it had all the more dollar-denominated liabilities.

The picture in Argentina, of course, is only the most dramatic. Throughout Latin America and throughout much of the world the prevalent view is that globalization and reform have failed. In countries like Bolivia people ask the question: "We have done everything that you told us to do. You were right that there would be a large amount of pain. We felt that pain, but when do we get the benefits?" And they are waiting. Not only do those in the developing countries see the policies that were imposed on them as ineffective. They also see an *unfair* agenda.

Bolivia, for instance, fought the drug war and eradicated the cocaine fields, which lowered their income significantly, but the United States maintained its high tariffs against Bolivia's products. Bolivia's exports of sugar into the United States are very restricted. Greater access to the American market could have compensated them for what they have done. They felt the pain, but saw little gain, and little attempt by America either to practice what it preaches in terms of free markets, or to reward them for their efforts on behalf of America's War on Drugs.

The long-term statistics for the region as a whole similarly give a bleak picture. The growth in the 1990s, the first full decade of the reform era, is just slightly better than half that in the pre-reform eras of the 1960s and 1970s. The unemployment rate is up three percentage points; the *percentage* of the population in poverty (on a $2 a day standard) is higher. Not surprisingly, then, the issue of the impact of reforms and globalization has become a topic of lively debate in Latin America.

Globalization: learning how to use it

The idea of globalization is very simple. The decrease of communication costs, transportation costs, and artificial barriers to goods and factors of production has led to a closer integration of the economies of the world. Globalization implies mobility not only of goods and services but also of capital and knowledge – and to a lesser extent of people. Globalization entails not only the integration of markets, but also the emergence of a global civil society.

The general thesis that I advance is that the most successful countries of the world have in effect partaken of globalization, they have used globalization, but they have done so on their own terms. The most successful countries in the world, notably those in East Asia, had growth that has been based on exports, which depended on globalization. But this growth involved gradual trade liberalization, not capital market liberalization – they did not open up their markets to speculative capital flows, at least in the critical early years. Many of the doctrines that were advanced by the IMF were simply wrong and counterproductive. The IMF, for instance, claimed that a country could not attract foreign investment unless it liberalized its capital market. That was wrong. The country that has been most successful in achieving foreign direct investment among the emerging markets, and is probably by now the number two in the world in terms of FDI, is China, and China has not opened up its capital markets to short-term speculative capital flows. It has gradually been liberalizing, but it has done so at its own pace. As a result, it has not suffered from the kinds of disasters that affected other countries in East Asia that liberalized under the influence (or pressure) of the IMF and the US Treasury.

The benefits of globalization that have been experienced by East Asia have included not only access to markets, but also access to more knowledge. What separates less developed and developed countries is not only a shortage of capital, but also a disparity in knowledge. The closing of the knowledge gap has been one of the important aspects of globalization. The closing of the knowledge gap not only allowed Korea to produce cars and chips that compete effectively with those produced in the most advanced industrial countries, but also has led to better health and longer lifespans throughout the world.

There have been other positive aspects of globalization: for instance, the globalization of civil society that brought about the Land Mines Treaty and the Jubilee Movement in the year 2002. The Jubilee Movement succeeded in achieving debt reduction for some of the most highly indebted poor countries. In the years I was at the World Bank, there was a program for debt relief for the highly indebted poor countries, but the IMF had to confirm whether the countries met the basic standards. It makes sense not to give relief to countries that make no efforts to use the money to advance development, but instead just squander the money. But the bar was set so high that virtually no country could meet it – about three countries did it in three years. As a result of the pressure that civil society placed through the Jubilee Movement, during the year 2000, more than 20 countries met the threshold. What happened was *not* that in that year all of a sudden countries around the world started behaving better. It was rather that it was at last recognized that the bar had been set at the wrong level, and civil society put pressure to adjust. A more reasonable perspective was adopted.

In many parts of the world, however, globalization has not been run by countries in ways that have enhanced their own welfare. The terms have been dictated by the outside. The result has been more poverty, more insecurity, more sense of voicelessness, weaker democracies, more volatility, weaker social fabric, reflected in many cases by more violence.

I was in an Indian village last year, in the high Andes, and had breakfast with the mayor of the village. The discussion reflected a keen awareness of how exchange rate changes affected their economy; and quickly turned to what was going to happen to the euro. I was struck, not only by their awareness of "globalization," but by how they had already picked up all the *Financial Times* vocabulary. That afternoon I went to another village and met with its mayor, and the discussion there was even more interesting. He explained to me the adverse effects of the neoliberal doctrines, and how IMF conditionality undermined democratic processes. He contended that traditional Indian practices of democratic participation provided an alternative approach, one that was more conducive to development. He also went on to describe in quite vivid terms how the 1994 WTO agreement had provided a framework under which bio-piracy was occurring; that international firms in particular were patenting traditional medicines and making it difficult for people in the villages to use them. I did not have a chance to assess the accuracy of what he was charging, but what it did bring home is that the issue of globalization and the issue of what happens in Geneva in the WTO is felt around the world.

There is a real phenomenon of globalization, which affects people everywhere in the world. It also highlights the fact that in these Indian villages the objection is not really to globalization, since some of their goods are being sold around the world and their incomes are rising as a result. Their access to health has improved. The objection is rather to the way globalization has been managed. In too many cases it has not been managed in ways that are in the interests of the developing countries, and especially of the poor in those countries.

Global governance without global government

Over the last 50 years, we have evolved a system of global governance without global government. I would like to make an analogy to what happened in the United States and other Western countries 150 years ago, when similar processes of declining transportation costs and communication costs were taking place, resulting in the formation of national economies. But when that occurred, there were national governments to manage that process and to make sure it worked well. In the United States, for instance, the first system of bank regulation, important for creating a strong national economy, was passed in 1863. Industrial policies, in the form of support for research and extension services in the agricultural sector (at the time the dominant sector of the economy), were also launched in the early 1860s. Even before that, the government had played an important role developing the telegraph network, just as it did more recently in the development of the internet. The first telegraph line was financed by the US government between Baltimore and Washington in 1842. So there is a long history of strong involvement of government in trying to help shape the economy.

At the global level, as the process of globalization has occurred, we have not had a similar structure of democratic governance that can help shape and guide that process. The system of global governance has some very serious problems, as I will stress later. But for now, I wish simply to observe that a consequence of this process of globalization is the increasing importance of global externalities and global public goods. The most important examples of this have already received much attention. The air pollution that occurs in one country can easily affect other countries. The emission of greenhouse gasses affects the atmosphere, and high levels of greenhouse emissions in the United States and other developed countries affect all the countries in the world, including the less developed ones. Terrorism that occurs in one country can have effects on others. Diseases in one country can spread across borders – they do not recognize political boundaries. Accordingly, we have a wide variety of contexts in which it is important to undertake global collective action, but we do not have political structures in which this action can be undertaken in a democratic way. The need for global collective action is particularly important in the context of development.

Unfair global agendas

The absence of democratic structures has resulted in trade rules and other rules that are unfair, in which policies tend more to reflect corporate and financial interests than the interests of the developing countries and the global economy more generally. The discrepancy between the rhetoric of the advanced industrial countries and their practices, including the rules that they fight so strongly for, exposes the developing countries to charges of hypocrisy, and undermines confidence in the whole process of globalization. Let me illustrate by means of a few examples.

Concerning the issue of unfair rules, the last round of trade negotiations, the Uruguay Round that was completed in 1994, was hailed as a great achievement, and indeed it was for the United States and for most of Western Europe. At the time, I was on the Council of Economic Advisors, and the Clinton Administration boasted about its positive effects on employment and incomes in America. But at the World Bank, we calculated also the impact on sub-Saharan African countries, the poorest in the world, and we found that their incomes would decrease by around 2 percent, because of terms of trade effects. Developed countries were insisting that the less developed countries open up their markets to their goods and eliminate subsidies, but the developed countries maintained their trade barriers against textiles and agricultural goods, and maintained the subsidies on their agricultural goods, that is precisely those goods that represented the comparative advantage of the developing world. For instance, US cotton subsidies, which exceed in amount the value of what is produced, so increase the supply of cotton, thereby depressing the international price, that income in several sub-Saharan countries is reduced by 1 to 2 percent *from this one subsidy alone*; the losses far exceed the value of American foreign assistance.

Compounding the discontent caused by this unfairness is the hypocrisy, evidenced recently by the increases in US farm subsidies and the imposition of steel tariffs. The United States claimed that it had the right to impose the tariffs as "safeguards." While the rest of the world questioned whether that was in fact the case, there was a more fundamental point: if the United States, the richest country in the world, with less than 6 percent unemployment even in the midst of a recession, with a reasonable safety net, claims it needs to impose tariffs to protect the relatively few workers who might lose their jobs, what are developing countries to think – countries where unemployment is high, where there are no safety nets, and where liberalization may cause massive job losses? Surely they too should be allowed to impose tariffs to protect their workers.

Another issue: one of the great achievements of the Uruguay Round was extending trade liberalization to services. But the services that were put on the agenda were financial services and information technology – the comparative advantage of the US, the UK and other advanced industrial countries. Other kinds of services, like maritime services and construction services, were kept off the agenda. These sectors were important to some developing countries. Again, the agenda for trade liberalization was set in a completely unfair way.

Special interests have been very important in determining the agendas of international economic negotiations in other areas as well. This was clear, for instance, in the case of intellectual property rights. Everybody recognizes the importance of intellectual property as an incentive to intellectual endeavor. More than 200 years ago, the United States Constitution, recognizing the importance of patents and copyrights in stimulating creative and innovative activity, specified this as one of the areas of federal responsibility. But we also recognize that intellectual property law is not natural law, it is man made and it has to balance the interests of the users and the producers. Within the White House, the Council of Economic Advisors and the Office of Science and Technology Policy argued that the intellectual property framework that was being put forward by the US Trade Representative in the negotiations in Geneva in 1993 and 1994, in the discussions of TRIPS (trade-related aspects of intellectual property rights), as the Uruguay Round of discussions was nearing the end, was inappropriate and unfair. We were worried about a number of aspects. For instance, we were worried that with this intellectual property framework, poor developing countries would not have access to life-saving drugs and as a result people would die. Signing that agreement was in effect signing a death warrant for those who would no longer be able to afford the drugs. Moreover, since the most important input to research is knowledge, an unbalanced intellectual regime could lead to an increase in the cost of the input to research and therefore it could actually slow down the pace of intellectual innovation. But the provisions that were finally adopted did not reflect the views of either the Office of Science and Technology Policy or the Council of Economic Advisors: they reflected the views of the pharmaceutical and drug companies and other corporate interests, who felt that the stronger the intellectual property protection the better. Balance was not something that concerned them.

The asymmetry between developed and developing countries is also evident in the question of countercyclical fiscal policy. Keynesian economics is alive and well everywhere among the developed countries, but developing countries are told to cut expenditures when they face an economic downturn. This is the wonderful medicine that was prescribed for Argentina. This country had a deficit, it was told by the IMF to cut expenditures, they did what they were told to do and GDP went down further, just as economic theory predicted. Argentina began from a worrisome 15 percent unemployment: under the IMF policies, open unemployment approached 20 percent, plus another 10–15 percent disguised unemployment. What is surprising about Argentina is not that riots broke out, but that it took so long.

The question I get over and over again is "why is it that in the North you believe in countercyclical policies, while in the South we are forced to have *pro-cyclical* policies?" And the same general principle holds in a whole variety of economic policies. In the North we are engaged in active debates about the nature of the reform of pension programs, the role of the government and the role of the private sector in providing protection for our old age. The prevalent view is that privatization of social security is not the solution. Yet the international institutions have been pushing privatization around the world. These are difficult issues on which reasonable people could differ, but it is important that there be a lively democratic debate about the course of action. Too frequently countries feel that they are not given that choice.

The pitfalls of capital market liberalization

The question of capital market liberalization – which was pushed both by the US Treasury and by the IMF – provides a good illustration of what is wrong in the existing governance system. In early 1993, the issue came up while I was at the Council of Economic Advisors. Korea had plans to liberalize its capital and financial markets. But from the point of view of the US Treasury the proposed pace of liberalization was too slow. The Council of Economic Advisors said that overwhelming evidence showed that there was a serious risk that rapid capital market liberalization would lead to economic instability. But the Treasury prevailed, and three years after the policy there was a crisis in Korea, as we had predicted.

One of the arguments for capital market liberalization is that the free flow of capital will improve economic efficiency and promote economic growth. It is remarkable that this view was pushed even though there was at the time (and is today) very little evidence that the free flow of capital would increase economic growth and there was at the time (reinforced by what has happened since) a considerable body of evidence that it would promote economic instability.

Another argument is often put forward: capital markets provide important discipline. Of course, democracy is also a disciplinary device: governments that do not perform well are supposed to lose elections. But even if someone does not trust democracy, and believes that some other disciplinarian is required, he or she should be very careful about which disciplinarian is chosen. Personally I do not like disciplinarians, but if you do, if you feel you *need* a disciplinarian, you should choose a disciplinarian that is not capricious and gives you the *right* discipline. In these terms, capital markets make poor disciplinarians: capital markets are capricious and often short-sighted. Capriciousness is evidenced by the volatility that characterizes capital markets. Moreover, short-term capital focuses on what will make money in the short term – not on what will lead to long-term growth. Think of what would happen if there was another kind of disciplinarian. Imagine that there was a free flow of skilled labor rather than a free flow of capital, and that skilled labor said, "Unless you provide the kind of environment that we like we'll leave." Governments would be forced to worry about environmental protection and the quality of the education in publicly provided schools. It would certainly be a very different kind of discipline than that provided by short-term capital markets.

Moreover, the cost to the economy of having capital markets provide these "disciplinarian" services can be enormous. This is shown clearly by the standard wisdom concerning prudential behavior on the part of governments when facing international capital markets. If a firm in a developing country were to borrow $100 million from an American bank, it would have to pay something like 18–20 percent interest. The dictates of prudential policy are that countries need to keep reserves in an amount at least equal to the amount of foreign denominated outstanding short-term loans. Thus, in our example, a country has to set aside $100 million in reserves. How do most countries keep those reserves? Most countries keep those reserves in US Treasury bills. That means that this poor country is borrowing from the United States, and paying 20 percent interest, and at the same time lending to the United States (when you buy a US Treasury Bill you are lending to the United States) at 2 percent. In effect this poor country is giving foreign aid to the United States amounting to $18 million a year. It is clear why the United States might like this, but it is very hard to see why this would be good for growth in the poor country.

Mismanaging the transition to a market economy

There have been more crises in the last quarter-century than ever before, and they have been deeper. Almost 100 countries had a crisis in little more than a quarter of a century. These crises were mismanaged. But the management of the transition from Communism to a market economy has been even worse. Today, Russia's GDP is a third below that at the beginning of the transition, while rates of poverty have gone from about 2 percent to somewhere between 20 and 40 percent, depending on how you measure it. A 1998 study of the World Bank showed that one out of two children were living in families in poverty. Most people thought that liberalizing and privatizing the Russian economy would have increased incomes, but a decade after the start of the transition that has not happened. Things have rather worsened.

The contrast between the transition in Russia and the transition in China is very marked. In the case of China, incomes have increased by 250 percent in the last decade and poverty has decreased. At the beginning of the decade, China's income was about 60 percent of Russia's; at the end of the decade, Russia's is about 60 percent of China's.

An agenda for reform

I have described a number of failures in the management of economic development, crises, and transitions, and the unfairness, the hypocrisy, the asymmetries that underlie many of these problems. What can be done to mitigate and redress those failures? I would like to propose a reform agenda comprising seven elements.

The first and most important item in the agenda is changing governance. The people making these decisions were intelligent, but as economists and political scientists we recognize that the decision-making structure affects the kind of decisions that are made, and in the international institutions there are a number of fundamental problems in this respect. The first fundamental problem is that of representation. When economic policies are made within developed countries, all the relevant parties are brought together in a cabinet meeting or sub-cabinet meeting. In the United States, each Administration has its own distinctive decision-making structure – in the Clinton Administration, decisions were vetted through what was called the National Economic Council, which brought together people from the Departments of Commerce, Justice, Labor, Treasury, from the Council of Economic Advisors, the US Trade Representative, and other parts of the government; when issues involving health are being discussed, the

Secretary of Health and Welfare is brought into the discussions; when issues involving the environment are being discussed, the head of the Environmental Protection Agency has a seat at the table. We argued about various policy options and all the stakeholders had a voice.

In the international arena, on the contrary, we have a system of what can be described as "silos." In the WTO, the negotiations are conducted by the trade ministers, and the environmental or labor ministers are not in the room when the discussions take place, even when the policies affect the environment or labor. When intellectual property was being discussed, neither the Office of Science and Technology Policy nor the Patent Office nor the Council of Economic Advisors nor the Secretary of Health and Welfare – all of whom could be affected by the decisions made, and many of whom had far more expertise in the issues associated with intellectual property – were direct participants in the negotiations.

The same thing is true with the IMF: the "governors" of the IMF are the finance ministers and central bank governors. And while the two sometimes do not see eye to eye, no one would claim that these represent a broad spectrum of opinions. In day-to-day management, matters are even worse; typically, the executive directors, who are responsible for oversight, are chosen by the finance ministries alone.

As the international economic institutions went about discussing the problems with the international economic architecture, guess who got invited to the table to redesign the table? The same people who were at the table. All too often, those people think that other participants would just confuse the discussions. In today's world, it should be unacceptable that so many of those who are affected by the policies have no direct voice in the decisions being made. If at issue were just payment clearance mechanisms between banks, then it would be reasonable to let the technical people make the decisions, but at issue in these international economic organizations are the rules of a game that affect every aspect of society. Yet the range of the decision-makers is very, very narrow.

The second, related issue concerns voting. Within our own democracies we accept the principle "one person, one vote." In the IMF and the World Bank, votes are allocated on the basis of some measure of economic wealth, but it is not even today's economic wealth: for years, it was the economic wealth as of the end of World War II, even though since then there has been an enormous change in the global economy. It is not surprising that with this distorted representation you get distorted outcomes. We often complain that in the UN Security Council five countries have a veto power for historical reasons. At the IMF, one country and one country alone has veto power. It is called the G1 and it is not shy about using that power. This must be changed, even though this change might not be possible in the short run.

But, as a third element in the agenda, there are other intermediate reforms that could make a big difference. Foremost among these is increasing openness. The more remote the political processes are from direct democratic accountability, the more important free access to information is. Within our democracies, we have legislation ensuring freedom of information, yet at the international level there is no Freedom of Information Act and citizens find it very difficult to know what is going on in the IMF. It is difficult even for their elected representatives. For instance, some time ago the US Congress passed a provision instructing the American Executive Director at the IMF to vote a particular way on a particular set of issues. The Executive Director did not follow those directions, but the vote was secret. It was only because these international institutions leak all the time that Congress found out that the US representative had voted in violation of the Congressional mandate.

The fourth element in my agenda for reform concerns the remit of the IMF. The IMF has broadened its mandate from focusing on crises to getting involved in transitions and development. It has not done a very good job in those other areas.

It undertook these new areas, even as it was failing in accomplishing its original mandate. It was set up under the intellectual influence of Keynes to encourage countries facing an economic downturn to have expansionary policies and to provide the liquidity with which they could finance those expansionary policies. Yet today the IMF insists that the countries to which it provides funds maintain a contractionary fiscal policy – just the opposite of what Keynes had in mind when he promoted the IMF.

By itself, narrowing the remit of the IMF will not solve the problem; the organization did a poor job in the East Asia crisis and in other crises. There has to be a change in the approach to crisis management. It is true that there have been some signs of progress recently, but it will need an enormous amount of pressure to push forward. The policy of big bailouts is being replaced (or at least its replacement is being discussed) by a policy of focusing on bankruptcies and standstills. When I argued for this position at the beginning of the East Asia crisis, people at the IMF said that bankruptcy amounted to reneging on a debt contract. In order to preserve the credit contract, the IMF all too often shredded the social contract. It found it acceptable to throw millions of people into unemployment and cut back food subsidies. The consequences were predictable and predicted. That was not only bad social policy but also bad economic policy, because the riots that broke out in countries like Indonesia devastated national economies.

Bankruptcy is actually part of any debt contract. Countries like Britain gave up debtor prisons a long time ago, and passed legislation allowing for bankruptcies, to give debtors a fresh start. In the nineteenth century, when Mexico failed to pay its debt obligations, the British and French armies moved in. Today the use of armies against countries that fail to pay their debts is no longer accepted, but some favor the use of economic coercion. Greater reliance on some form of bankruptcy and standstills, instead of the big bailouts which have proved so ineffective, often leaving the countries only more indebted, is a reform long overdue.

The fifth element of the agenda is broadening surveillance. One of the things that the IMF does today is to go into a country and say, "we experts on economic management think that you ought to change the way you are managing your economic policy in such and such a way." The Fund is supposed to provide peer pressure. The surveillance originated as the Article IV consultation, that is, consultation to make sure that the country was complying with the articles it had agreed to in joining the IMF. But as mission creep occurred in other areas, this too expanded from what was supposed to be a review ensuring compliance with the articles of agreement to a very broad-based surveillance that includes virtually all aspects of macroeconomic activity.

I saw that kind of surveillance in the case of the United States. The IMF suggested that inflation was about to break out in the United States. This was because, according to the Fund, if unemployment ever got below 6.2 percent, then inflation increased. On the basis of our own analysis, we had concluded that this was not correct, and we ignored their recommendation. We were right, they were wrong. Unemployment decreased to 3.9 percent and we still had no increase in inflation. There had been changes in the structure of our economy and in the global economy that allowed this to happen. This case shows that the IMF not only had its economics wrong, it also focused too narrowly on a single objective, inflation. When we decided on our economic policy, we were concerned with unemployment as part of a broader social policy. We recognized that if we got our unemployment rate down, welfare dependency would decrease and the crime rate would decrease as well. These concerns never even entered the minds of the people implementing the Article IV consultation – or at least it did not seem to be the case in what they reported.

It is important to broaden the range of surveillance to include concerns such as decent work and employment, which are the focus of the International Labour Organization. I am not arguing for an elimination of IMF surveillance, but its reports should be only one piece of information among several that influence the economic decision-making of countries.

The sixth element of reform I want to emphasize is the need to put more effort into strengthening democracy. Many of the policies that have been pursued by the IMF and other institutions have undermined democracy by imposing conditionality and thus narrowing the set of policy options.

Finally, one of the most important aspects of globalization is the recognition of the growing importance of global public goods and externalities. I have time here to present just one example. If there are places – say, the Cayman Islands – where money laundering can occur, this affects other countries directly, because illegal activity in other countries gets laundered through bank accounts there. The OECD recognized the public-good nature of this issue and a year ago drafted a treaty that was meant to reduce the opportunity for this kind of activity to occur. Before September 11, the US Treasury vetoed it. After September 11, it was recognized that those same centers were also the centers through which terrorists were funded. These secret bank accounts not only help support trafficking in drugs, tax evasion, and terrorism, but also adversely affect development: huge amounts of money, much of it related to corruption, are, for instance, flowing out of Africa, and to a large extent this is made possible by these offshore banking centers to which people can bring money they stole from their country. The existence of these offshore banking centers provides a *negative externality* to other countries; there is a need for collective action at a global level.

We need to have ways of financing global public goods as well as controlling global externalities. There are a variety of ways that might be considered. One source of finance entails an expansion of a framework that has already been decided upon: Special Drawing Rights (SDRs). There is a need for the emission of additional liquidity to offset the money that is being put into reserves every year. If those SDR emissions occurred every year and were used to finance global public goods, and in particular development, it could provide a source of funding that would not depend on the vagaries of the national parliaments in particular countries.

A second potential source of funding is associated with the management of the global commons. These are global natural resources such as seabed minerals, fisheries, Antarctica, and our atmosphere. If the revenues generated from the management of these global resources were used to help finance global public goods, we would have another assured financial basis to address the externalities produced by globalization.

Concluding remarks

The agenda of globalization and development is a broad one. Today, there are few issues of greater importance. Globalization does have enormous potential for promoting economic development. But because of the way globalization has proceeded over the last 50 years, it has not lived up to that potential. There are reforms that can be made. Some of them are difficult, but others are clearly feasible. As we enter into this new century, it is important that we reform the globalization process, to ensure that it will live up closer to its potential to improve the lives and livelihoods of those in the developing world.

Note

1 Many of the ideas in this lecture are developed at greater length in Joseph E. Stiglitz, *Globalization and its Discontents* (New York and London: W. W. Norton, 2002). See also the speeches collected in *The Rebel Within: Joseph Stiglitz and the World Bank*, ed. Ha-Joon Chang (London: Anthem Press, 2001). For basic data on development, see the annual World Bank *World Development Reports*, *World Economic Indicators* and *Global Economic Prospects*.

3

Globalizing Justice

Robert E. Goodin

Economists, with notable exceptions, have been having a persist-
ently pernicious influence all around the world of late. The reason
is their constitutional incapacity to keep markets in their place,
under proper political control.

Even Chicago economists know deep down that some things
can be bought and sold only on condition that other things are
not. So, for example, there is no point in buying *title* to property
if it would be cheaper to buy off the police and the judges who are
supposed to be enforcing claims to property titles.

In recent years, the World Bank has been railing most usefully
against corruption.[1] It has been promoting a strong state, in *that*
sense, as a necessary concomitant of the market. But there remains
far too little appreciation in that quarter of the need to make sure
that other things, besides public officials, are protected from
marketeering.

It is not just a matter of preventing the buying and selling of
people (though in some corners of the world the slavery conventions could still do with a fair bit more enforcement). It is more
fundamentally a matter of preventing the buying and selling of
things *dear* to people. It is a matter of preventing the corrosive
influence of the market from diminishing the *value* of things in the
process of allocating them 'efficiently'.

In our personal lives, each of us tries to keep certain spheres safely sequestered from crass commercial considerations. (Richard Titmuss's famous example was the gift of blood.)[2] So too do we as a nation try to keep some of our fundamental collective decisions safely sequestered from undue influence by others. Different people and peoples value the opportunity to do things differently.

That capacity to do things differently, here from elsewhere, is precisely what old-fashioned trade barriers used to buy us. And that is what is lost with the collapse of those trade barriers and rampant globalization.

Or so economists allege, anyway. Now, I am no expert in international economics. But I do not think that you need to be to see that the wilder claims of globalization just must be false.

Simple experiments are often the most telling. The best I know came in the course of the commission to enquire why the space shuttle *Challenger* fell from the sky. Experts from the National Aeronautics and Space Administration (NASA) were called to testify. They were asked, 'Could the freezing air temperatures have cracked the rubber "o-rings" connecting stages of the rocket, causing the crash?' NASA officials replied, 'Don't know: haven't done the relevant experiments yet.' At that point Nobel Laureate physicist Richard Feynman (certainly the funniest and probably the smartest member of the commission) piped up, 'Allow me.' He picked up the o-ring material lying on the witness table, plunged it in the ice water in front of him, pulled it out, banged it on the table, and watched it shatter – and with it, NASA's credibility for years to come.

Here is a corresponding globalization experiment. Go to your closet. Look at the labels in your shirts. If globalization is true, why don't *all* the labels say 'Made in China'? (Indeed, why do *none* of them say 'Burkina Faso', where unit labour costs are even lower?) Go to the kitchen. Up-end your favourite half dozen appliances. If globalization is true, why do *any* of them say 'Made in Germany', where unit labour costs are so high?

This informal evidence is backed up by rafts of careful empirical work suggesting that the wilder claims of globalization ('hyper-globalization', as it is sometimes called) are indeed unsustainable.[3] The fact of the matter seems to be that individual states have more room for independent manoeuvre than hyperglobalizationists would imply. But those are issues for others – empirical political scientists and economists – to resolve.

Here I intend to address issues of globalization as a philosopher, with no special claim to empirical expertise. So for the remainder of this chapter I shall, purely for the sake of argument, assume that the facts of the matter are precisely as hyperglobalizationists allege them to be. Let's assume, for the sake of argument, that the world really is just one big marketplace, characterized by friction-less factor mobility and perfectly free trade in perfectly interchange-able commodities. As I say, I cannot imagine that that is completely true, and I suspect that it may not be even remotely true. But suppose it is. What would follow?

I ask that question from the perspective of a *moral* philosopher. My concern is with what difference, if any, globalization might make to the theory and practice of social morality. Would glob-alization be good news or bad news, from a moral point of view?

That larger question resolves itself into two component ques-tions, potentially quite distinct from one another. One is the 'in principle' question. How would globalization sit with the *basic structure* of morality? Is it possible, even in principle, that global-ization might be good news, morally? Second is the 'in practice' question. Assuming globalization could in principle be morally good news, how (if at all) can that moral potential actually be realized, in practice?

Principles, of course, constitute the moral philosopher's stock in trade. But moral philosophers ignore issues of practice very much at their peril. Moral choice, like any choice, inevitably repres-ents the intersection of desirability considerations and feasibility considerations. Desirable though something may be in principle, it is all just pie in the sky unless you can find some effective way of implementing it.[4]

A central tenet of institutional design which I urge upon my fellow moral philosophers is the proposition that *'mechanisms matter'*.[5] Accordingly, I conclude this chapter with a 'laundry list' of mechanisms by which globalization might – just might – be put in the service of the moral community.

Showing how globalization might be made moral is not to guarantee that it will be. But revealing possibilities is an important first step towards realizing them. Some diffuse sense that 'there is no alternative' (TINA, in Thatcher-speak) often serves to reconcile us to all sorts of unsatisfactory arrangements. But we remain reconciled only so long as that assumption remains unstated and unexamined, far in the background. Once the proposition is put squarely on the table, the claim is open to genuine scrutiny, in the course of which such TINA claims can usually be exposed for the frauds that they usually are.

In principle

Before turning to ways and means, let us first consider ends. As a moral philosopher, the ends I have in view are *ethical* ends: matters of The Right and The Good. The question that concerns me is whether, from the point of view of The Right and The Good, globalization is good news or bad.

At one level the answer seems straightforward. If there are any truths of morality at all, then surely they are universal (which is to say, *global*) truths. No doubt morality contains some optional extras; and no doubt there are various equally good ways of filling in even some of its most essential details. But at some suitable level of generality, the truths of morality must surely be the same everywhere. The truths of morality – if truths there be – surely are not indexed to time and place, any more than are the truths of mathematics. We do not say '2 plus 2 equals 4, *around here*.'

71

Neither do we say, 'It's wrong to murder and maim people, *around here*.'

Shortly I shall provide a little more nuance to that bald universalist claim. But what I want to note first, and most firmly, is just this. If you take the traditional sort of view that I do that morality is universal, then having a socio-economic regime like globalization that has a similarly universal reach is at least *potentially* a good thing, too.

Of course, potentiality is one thing, actuality another. Globalization will actually be a good thing, morally, just if (just because; just in so far as) that universalizing socio-economic regime can be made to track universal morality. People who are wary of globalization worry on precisely that score, and that is a worry to which I return in the second section of this chapter.

What I want to note first and foremost just *is* the structural isomorphism. If you think of morality in universal terms, then other social forces that operate in the same universalizing fashion should in principle be good news rather than bad.

Having asserted the claims of universalist morality rather boldly, let me now try to assuage the ghost of Ernest Gellner. Contrary to what he might have thought, I am not asking anyone to sign on to some monotheist cult, or a form of philosophical foundationalism that serves as its academically respectable equivalent.[6]

My argument can be rendered perfectly consistent with a purely *constructivist* understanding of morality. To do so, you just have to suppose that, while morality is indeed socially conventional, what it is a socially constructed solution *to* is a set of problems which have to be faced by *all* societies, and to which there is a *limited* set of socially stable solutions.

If that is so, then the problems of living together will drive everyone, everywhere, to broadly the same solutions – to socially construct broadly the same sets of fundamental rules for themselves. Different societies might fill in the details a little differently; but the basic rules are likely to be socially constructed in pretty much the same way, pretty much everywhere.

The trick to finding this common core of universal morality is to pitch the description at the suitable level of generality – general enough to be universal, but specific enough to have some useful practical content.

That is the trick that Amartya Sen and Martha Nussbaum (and the World Bank following them) hope to pull off with their talk of 'capabilities'.[7] Different people in different places might put their capacities to different particular uses; but the same basic capabilities (life, liberty and empowerment in various dimensions) will be needed whatever the particular uses to which they are subsequently put. This is the same trick that John Rawls pulled off (more successfully I think than he himself subsequently thought) in talking about 'primary goods' – things that are necessary preconditions, whatever else one cares to accomplish.[8]

All those are ways of showing how The Good might be morally universal – the same for everyone, everywhere – despite the great diversity of particular goods that different people in different places might pursue. The same strategy can be used to show how The Right might be morally universal – the same for everyone, everywhere – despite the diversity of particular different rights and duties that are imposed on, and by, different peoples in different places. Henry Shue persuasively argues that rights to physical security and subsistence are 'basic rights', in the same Rawlsian sense of being necessary preconditions for *any* other rights or duties you might have. Security and subsistence are basic rights, Shue argues, because they are logically required to underwrite the sort of human *agency* that is presupposed by any other more specific rights or duties.[9]

In these sorts of ways, I think we can (at a suitable level of generality, at least) produce a list of human rights that has a credible claim to universal application. It is not just the old Roman *jus gentium*, a list of rights that legal codes all across the world *happen* to have in common.[10] (The trouble with that approach is that the moment some crazy state somewhere strikes off a right from its domestic statute books, that right necessarily falls out of the *jus gentium* as well.) What I have in mind is not just an 'overlapping consensus' of that purely contingent sort. Instead, the universal human rights derived in my preferred way are right whether or not everyone (or *in extremis*, anyone) currently respects them.

It is easy enough to persuade most people of that proposition, at least in part. Of course there are always obdurate postmodernists prepared to deny *any* truths. But most people are usually prepared to agree that there is a common core of moral minimalism – the negative rules of 'Thou Shalt Not' morality – that *do* have universal application. Most people are prepared to believe that we ought not to murder, maim or torture people, whether or not they are 'one of us'.[11]

Whether we are under any *positive* moral obligation actually to *help* people who are 'not one of us' is often regarded as quite another matter. 'Commonsense morality' of an unreflective sort almost always tends to assume that our duties towards strangers in general, and foreigners most especially, are almost entirely of the negative ('do no harm') sort. Commonsense morality tends to assume that it is only towards people with whom we have some 'special relationship' that we have any particularly strong positive duties to help.

Philosophers are famous for crazy examples. Here is one of the most famous. Suppose your house is on fire. Suppose you have time to rescue only one of the two people who are trapped inside. Suppose one of them is Archbishop Fénelon, a great benefactor to mankind. Suppose the other is your own mother. In such a case, commonsense morality insists, surely it *must* be right to rescue your mother in preference to Archbishop Fénelon – and in so doing, to let personal relationships take priority over the demands of abstract, impersonal morality.[12]

Utilitarian philosophers rail mightily against that conclusion, of course. 'What magic is there in the pronoun, "my" that should justify us in overturning the dictates of impartial reason?', roared William Godwin – the eighteenth-century anarchist and utilitarian, partner of Mary Wollstonecraft, father of Mary Shelley and hence grandfather of Frankenstein.[13] But rail though utilitarians might, commonsense morality remains firm in its conclusion that special relationships matter more than impersonal morality, in these sorts of cases – and, by extension, that fellow citizens ought to matter more than distant strangers in our moral calculations.

For my own part, of course, I am on the side of Frankenstein. But it does no good for us utilitarian, universalist cosmopolitans *merely* to rail. It does no good simply to say, 'I just do not see what possible difference a tie of blood (much less mere national-ity) might make, morally.' The 'I just don't see . . .' ploy is like an exposed argumentative chin, inviting the caustic jab in reply, 'Is that a criticism or a confession?'

If we want to defend the claim that the demands of morality are at root universal, despite superficial appearances to the contrary, what we universalists must do is offer critics some account of *why* superficial appearances seem otherwise. What sort of story can we tell to square our universalism with the firm commonsense intuition that we owe people in special relationships to us (like our mothers) more, by way of positive assistance, than we owe to people (even morally very worthy people, like Archbishop Fénelon) who stand in no such special relationship to us?

It is not hard to find such a story. All that we moral universalists have to do is to point to the advantages of a moral division of labour.[14] In morality just as in economics, specialization has its advantages. More good gets done when some people concentrate on one thing, and some on another, than when everybody tries to do everything at once. In the case of the positive personal assist-ance here in view, people who are closest to hand are usually the best situated to *know* what is needed, and they are usually the best able to *act efficaciously* to do what is needed.

If all that is true, then it obviously follows that moralists who are in principle universalists would in practice divide up the moral chores, and assign special responsibility for particular people to other particular people, typically those who are physically proximate to them. That gives rise to morally 'special relation-ships' within families, on the one hand, and within nations, on the other. The superficial structure of social morality will thus *seem* particularist – it would allow us (indeed, require us) to favour those who are known and near to us over distant strangers. But the deep structure of morality will remain universalist, through and through.

The deep structure matters, though. Here is why. If the super-ficial particularism went all the way down, then we would *never* have any reason to provide positive assistance to anyone who was *not* 'one of us'. All we would ever owe them would be the negat-ive 'Thou Shalt Not' duties of moral minimalism.

That is *not* true, however, if the particularism is merely on the surface of everyday morality. Suppose that that particularism is in fact underpinned by universalist duties, which have merely been assigned to particular people. Then everyone has at least a *residual* duty ('residual', in the sense of 'left over' from the uni-versal duty we all had, before any special duties got assigned to anyone) to make sure that those special duties *are* discharged – in the first instance, by the particular person to whom they have been assigned; but failing that, by the moral community *at large*, acting through any of many other potential agents.

This is the fundamental premise of the international law of refugees, for one particularly topical example. Whatever may be the ordinary priority of your duty to render positive assistance first and foremost to your own (in this case, your own fellow countryfolk), if there are people who for whatever reason stand outside this ordinary system of protection – people without a coun-try; or people whose fellow countryfolk cannot or will not help them, or actively threaten to harm them – then a residual duty falls to the moral community at large to assist such persons *as if* they were one of our own. That is the law of refugees, from Grotius and before.[15]

Of course, that is a duty that the whole moral community world-wide shares, and if any one country does it then no other will need to. So the situation naturally invites attempts at buck-passing and free-riding. (Contemporary history is full of examples of that.) But that is just to say that some mechanism is needed to assign special responsibility for discharging these *secondary, residual* responsibilities which we can deploy in case of a breakdown in the system of special first-order responsibilities assigned on the basis of things like proximity and nationality.

My point here is simply that, when we look at special responsibilities (towards parents and compatriots and so on) as merely *universal* duties that have been *assigned* to particular people, then there remain these residual duties – universal in the first instance – to ensure that the people to whom they have been assigned actually discharge them, and to do something about it ourselves if they do not.

If I am right about that, then it is not only refugees to whom we owe a positive duty of rescue. Refugees are a very special and important case, no doubt. But what is special about them is not just that they have happened to have washed up on our doorstep. Surely what is crucial in activating our residual duties towards refugees – and lots of others as well – is the fact that those who originally had been assigned primary responsibility for helping them are now unable or unwilling to do so.

Many people around the world, not just refugees, find themselves in that unhappy situation. And if we have a residual duty to protect anyone and everyone in that situation, worldwide, then that provides a powerful argument for coordinated international assistance. On that analysis, the First World ought to provide aid to the Third, simply because governments there are unable to 'take care of their own' without such outside assistance.

In practice

Before turning to some practical suggestions for how to implement such international transfers, let us first revisit the theme of globalization and how it might impact on morality in the international sphere.

So far I have concentrated exclusively on the 'in principle' issue. Globalization might be a morally good thing, at least in principle, because its universalizing tendencies line up nicely with the universalism of morality itself. Universalist, cosmopolitan moralists like me say that (at some suitable level of generality) the same rules should apply to everyone, everywhere. Globalization, we are told, will have precisely that universalizing effect. In principle, that looks like a happy coincidence.

Just how happy that coincidence turns out to be, in practice, will depend entirely on *which* rules globalization imposes universally. According to the conventional wisdom, globalization imposes the rules of the market; and the rules of the unfettered market are all too often diametrically at odds with the rules of true morality.

That has indeed been the way of globalization so far. Whether that is *necessarily* so, or whether there might be some room for moral manoeuvre within the structure of globalization, is the 'in practice' question to which I now turn.

First, some diagnostics.

What worries us about globalization is that it deprives us of our old, familiar ways of pursuing social justice. Universalist and cosmopolitan though their moral principles might be, in practice campaigners for social justice have (with a few honourable exceptions) almost invariably tended to pursue The Right and The Good 'one country at a time'.[16]

Usually they do so slightly apologetically. In concentrating on securing as much social justice as they can in their *own* country, and letting global justice take care of itself, they do so more as a matter of prudence than of principle. They know all too well just how hard it is to achieve justice, even in *one* jurisdiction. They suppose (not unreasonably) that if they had to achieve justice everywhere at once in order to achieve it anywhere at all then their task would be utterly hopeless.

That is how trade barriers were surprisingly defended by none other than John Maynard Keynes, in a 1933 essay arguing for 'National self-sufficiency':

> We ... need to be as free as possible from interference from economic changes elsewhere, in order to make our own favourite experiments towards the ideal social republic of the future; and ... movement towards greater national self-sufficiency and economic isolation will make our task easier ...[17]

We can see clearly enough how that might be useful in promoting social justice at *home*. Notice, however, that it might *also* have been a good strategy for promoting social justice worldwide, provided certain further assumptions were met.

'Compartmentalized cosmopolitanism', as I shall call it, offers a positive, unapologetic defence of the strategy of pursuing justice 'one country at a time'. The basic precepts of that strategy are these:

1   Do as much Good as you can, at home.
2   Do no harm, abroad.
3   Then – just so long as the moral division of labour works the way it is supposed to – that will maximize the amount of Good that gets done, worldwide.

Of course, that appeal to the 'moral division of labour' overlooks the unwritten clause, which I have just been emphasizing, about 'back-up responsibilities'. But set that to one side. This model of 'compartmentalized cosmopolitanism' has further vulnerabilities all its own.

The strategy of compartmentalized cosmopolitanism assumes, first, that the compartments are watertight: that nothing we do in pursuit of justice within our country will impact, positively or negatively, on the pursuit of justice within any other country. In that case (but *only* in that case) pursuing maximal justice in *each* place can lead to maximal justice in *every* place.

That assumption of watertight compartments might have been true at some time in the past. But it is true no longer. Cross-boundary spillovers – political and moral, as well as economic and environmental – are now absolutely endemic.

A second crucial assumption underwriting the strategy of compartmentalized cosmopolitanism is that we can act more effectively at close quarters than we can at a distance. Our information is better, our networks are denser, our capacity to bring pressure is greater, and so on.

Again, all that was once true, but it is true no longer. Most of us probably now know more about what is happening in Paris or Brussels or New York than we do about what is happening in some medium-sized city a fraction of the distance away (Leeds, say, for Londoners). Just as knowledge at a distance is now easier, so too is *action* at a distance. When Australian environmentalists wanted to stop a dam on a particularly beautiful Tasmanian river, they found it easier to appeal to the UN World Heritage Site listing rather than to the consciences of Tasmanian legislators.

The upshot is that 'compartmentalized cosmopolitanism' – focusing on 'justice in one country', and trusting that that will best promote justice all around – may once have been a viable strategy, but it is no longer. It is no longer morally permissible to pursue domestic justice without any regard for transnational consequences. Nor is it practically possible, in a globalized world, to pursue policies that are *very* different, one place from another.

The bad news from a moral point of view is that all the progress we have made towards justice, domestically, is now at risk of being undermined from abroad. If claims of hyperglobalization are true, we can no longer have 'islands of justice in a sea of injustice'. If claims of hyperglobalization are true, we cannot secure justice among ourselves without securing justice for everyone else worldwide.

From the perspective of *universal* morality, however, that surely should be good news, at least of a sort. Hyperglobalization would give us (in the hackneyed courtroom formula) both the motive and the opportunity to attack social justice on a grander scale. We merely need to be a little more creative in thinking about what mechanisms to employ when it is no longer just a matter of mounting a campaign for domestic political leadership (although we should obviously still do that, too: in part to promote local justice in a less completely globalized world, and in part to activate transnational mechanisms for pursuing global justice discussed below).

Here are some illustrative suggestions of how we might pursue truly *global* social justice in an increasingly globalized world. They are no more than a 'laundry list' of a few possible mechanisms. There undoubtedly are others; others are quite probably better. This list is merely illustrative.

International treaty regimes

International treaty regimes are perhaps the most familiar, and historically the most influential, mechanisms of international social protection.

We in the industrialized West tend these days to take for granted the great gains of the International Labour Organization.[18] But in the poorer countries of the world, where sweatshops are still as endemic as cholera, the ILO is still a great force for good. So too is the World Health Organization, as we increasingly come to realize that the best way of improving people's health is by improving people's standard of living more generally: the best inoculation against a great many diseases of poverty is an injection of hard, cold cash. And even those great holding companies of international capital, the OECD and the World Bank, have recently begun pressing for minimal standards of living.

My interest here is not so much in those particular organizations as in the basic strategic option that they represent. What all those organizations have in common is that they are based on multilateral treaties among member states.

Now, we ordinarily tend to think of treaties as flimsy things. The reasons are obvious. In acceding to treaties, states can and often do stipulate 'reservations', thus exempting themselves from some of the more onerous obligations of the treaty. Furthermore, accession is rarely irreversible; usually states can, with due notice, simply withdraw from the treaty. Self-styled political realists therefore tend to suppose that treaties are pretty weak chains for binding strong states determined to behave badly.

Here as usual, however, realpolitik turns out actually to be pretty *un*realistic. It is really rather rare for states to withdraw from treaty regimes, once they are in them. (The present patch of US history is distinctly odd, in that and many other respects.) The reason states hesitate to withdraw from treaties is that treaties, like contracts (which are their domestic analogues), work to the benefit of all parties. Everyone gets something out of them, in one way or another; and those are things they could get *only* by being in, and staying in, the relationship. Furthermore, the longer you are in the relationship the more intertwined your affairs become, and the harder it is for you to withdraw. So even though it might formally seem as if treaty regimes have no real power over member states, the informal reality is that they typically provide an awful lot of leverage.

Notice, finally, that treaty regimes often start small and grow. Just think of the European Union. It started out as a miserable little European Coal and Steel Community. It fluffed around for fully two decades over little more than labour mobility within the European Economic Community. But in politics, one thing leads to another. 'Harmonization' is the most magical word in EU-speak; and among the things that most obviously need to be 'harmonized', in order to ensure a level playing field for employers across the EU, are the 'social wages' (welfare benefits) paid to workers in member states. And while we are not quite there yet, it is pretty clear that some such ratcheting-up dynamic might lead, before long, to the EU's becoming (in fact if not in name) the first transnational welfare state.[19]

Transnational networks and NGOs

Treaty regimes are thus one set of mechanisms through which we might pursue social justice on a more global scale. Another works in the interstices of those treaty regimes. I am thinking, here, of transnational networks and NGOs – non-governmental organizations. Transnational networks are more informal alliances among like-minded activists in different countries; NGOs, as the name implies, are more formally institutionalized.[20] Both, however, work in much the same way.

Consider the example of international human rights.[21] The formal treaty regime – the UN Declaration and associated conventions, and the various other subject- or region-specific declarations and treaties – creates the institutional site at which all this activity occurs. But once that basic apparatus is in place, what drives social change is basically just networking among activists. Within Kenya itself, for example, human rights activists might not have much clout. But, like Peer Gynt, they just go round-about. They get on to their chums in Africa Watch, who get on to their chums in Amnesty International, who in turn put pressure on governments in Britain or Sweden or wherever to put pressure on Kenya.

The same happens in campaigns for international environmental protection. Environmental NGOs lobby corporations, convincing them that reducing pollution is good business in various ways; and they in turn lobby governments.[22] Or, again, foreign NGOs work through US-based NGOs to pressure the American government. And so on. Eventually, Greenpeace experts work themselves into sufficiently central positions in these networks that they get appointed as official delegates of various national governments to international meetings; and important treaties (like the Bamako Convention on Transboundary Movement and Management of Hazardous Wastes) end up getting drafted literally in the Greenpeace office.[23] In short, networking works.

Similar strategies can be deployed in pursuit of global justice more generally. The downtrodden can appeal over the heads of

Robert E. Goodin

their own national governments, if those are unwilling or unable to help them, to the world community more generally. Through the good offices of transnational networks willing to 'put pressure for the poor', those appeals can have real force.

Mere networks, like treaties, may *look* like pretty flimsy affairs from a realpolitik perspective. Non-governmental organizations, by definition, lack the power of the state to punish and to reward. All they have is the power to petition – to talk, and to embarrass. Those may seem paltry powers. But before dismissing them entirely, recall that that is the principal mechanism by which business gets done among states themselves. Our image of international talking-shops like the UN may be as sites of stonewalling, places where nothing ever gets done, where talking *intentionally* replaces doing. And that might well be true of lots of deliberations, in the UN and elsewhere.

But look at the things that *do* get done, internationally. The *way* that they get done is by working things out, over a moderately protracted period, within 'webs of dialogue'. Anyone who doubts it need simply go to Geneva, where one of the major trade blocs that lobbies the World Trade Organization takes its very *name* (the Boeuf Rouge Group) from the restaurant where its representatives regularly meet.[24] States in the Boeuf Rouge Group know that talk matters. The rest of us should listen.

States resort to the *unique* state resources of threats and coercion only absolutely *in extremis* – and even then, often to no particularly powerful effect. More often, they come to 'understandings', largely tacit and informal, substantially unenforceable in any formal legal sense.[25] In all these respects, the informal power of transnational networks and non-governmental organizations merely to cajole seems to be perfectly on a par with the real way that states most typically exercise their power – the swaggering of realpolitik theoreticians notwithstanding.

International taxes and transfers

A third and more visionary mechanism by which we might pursue global justice would be through formal systems of international taxes and transfers. Various ones have been proposed over the years.

One is the 'resource tax'.[26] Its underlying principle is enormously appealing. 'God gave the earth to mankind in common,' says Locke.[27] And what he *should* have gone on to say (but didn't) is that nature's bounty should therefore belong to the world at large, rather than to any particular people who plopped themselves down on some particular patch and had the audacity to proclaim 'This is mine!'[28]

Appealing though the principle may be, in practice a resource tax seems politically doomed. Winners and losers can identify themselves all too clearly from the outset when it comes to taxing resources already owned. When you talk about levying an 'energy tax' on oil or coal extraction, for example, Texas oilmen know exactly how much they stand to lose, and they lobby their friend in the White House accordingly. The coal men do the same to his Australian counterpart. The upshot is an unholy transnational alliance, all across the world, to block any substantial tax on energy resources.

Politically, the only remotely promising strategy is to impose an international tax on resources of the world that are as yet unclaimed. Among the ones that have been mentioned in this connection, at one time or another, are minerals on the bed of the deep seas; 'wavebands' for broadcasting and communications; and 'slots' for geostationary orbits above the earth.[29] The idea behind a 'resource tax', here, would be to vest property rights in those resources in (say) some agency of the UN which would then auction them off to the highest bidders, redistributing the proceeds to the poorer countries of the world.

Still, some people will suppose that even seizing property from no one is more than the UN is up to. The world being what it is, they may well be right. So let me pass quickly over the many interesting variations on those proposals, and skip straight to the one transnational tax that I think should be politically the easiest to sell: the Tobin tax.

The problem which the Tobin tax was originally supposed to solve was the problem of too many petrodollars sloshing around from one country to another,[30] wreaking havoc with national economies in the process. The idea has been resurrected more recently as a solution to the problem of currency speculators shifting their money madly from one country to another, in search of a quick buck. Tobin's idea was to put a little 'sand in the wheels of international finance' by introducing a small tax, payable every time you converted money from one currency to another. Even a very tiny percentage tax would, we are told, be sufficient to erase the speculative gains that drive the most destructive sorts of international financial volatility.

It would also, incidentally, generate an enormous amount of tax revenues. But those revenues are wholly incidental. The benefits for the international financial system derive purely from the tax being collected, and do not at all depend on how the tax monies are subsequently spent. You can give their money to the poor; you can give it to the UN; you can give it to Greenpeace; you can burn it or bury it or dump it in the ocean. The benefits that Tobin has in mind for the international financial system are the same, no matter.

This creates a deliciously win-win situation. The rich countries of the First World are among the principal beneficiaries of having a Tobin tax imposed. (I hardly need remind a British audience of the pernicious effects on the national economy of 'Zurich gnomes' or, more recently, of George Soros betting against the pound.) The poor countries of the Third World are potentially among the principal beneficiaries of how the tax money is most likely to be spent, on any of many current proposals. (The Copenhagen UN Social Development Summit's proposal was the most explicitly pro-poor; but many of the places that would benefit most from

UN peacekeeping or expenditures on sustainable development are also in the poorest regions of the Third World.) Thus, on the face of things, it looks as if it should be possible to mobilize a broad coalition between the First World and the Third behind a Tobin tax.

Notice now one other interesting feature of a Tobin tax. Some international mechanisms work only if every country in the world adopts them. In those cases, the coordination problem is large and the chances of success are slim. Other international mechanisms, in contrast, work perfectly well with only a few key players on board.

One example of that is international environmental protection. As George Kennan argued long ago, if the twenty countries that were the heaviest polluters in the world could get together and limit their emissions, that would make a major difference to world pollution – regardless of what the rest of the world did.[31] The 1987 Montreal Protocol for preventing ozone depletion was built on precisely that proposition: it stipulated that it would come into force once ratified, not by some fixed number of countries (as is standard for international agreements), but rather by some weighted proportion of the heaviest emitters of greenhouse gasses.[32]

The Tobin tax is, I suggest, another example of an international regime that could work without the cooperation of absolutely every country in the world. It would work perfectly well just so long as (say) the top twenty trading nations were party to the regime. Of course, people could always then avoid the Tobin tax by holding their financial reserves in some other currency: escudos or pesos or bahts or whatever. But the risks associated with dodgy currencies would presumably make that a relatively untempting option.

Of course, getting the Swiss on board is always going to be tricky. More generally, there is always a great incentive to try to be the one country with a reliable currency that is not in the Tobin tax regime. I do not mean to trivialize the hard politics that will be required to overcome the temptations of gaming in such situations. By the same token, we ought not to exaggerate those obstacles – which are frankly no different in kind from any of a range of other temptations that inevitably threaten to stand in the way of international cooperation on virtually any topic. Bluffs can be called, pressure brought to bear: the international community knows how to do that, whenever its mind is sufficiently concentrated.[33] Even the Swiss eventually coughed up the Third Reich booty, after all.

Among these three sorts of mechanisms for pursuing social justice on a global scale, the one that I find most attractive is, obviously, the Tobin tax. But either of the other mechanisms – international treaty regimes, or formal or informal transnational networks – might work equally well. In the very short term, they would probably work even better.

This list of mechanisms is not exhaustive, merely a sample. These examples establish what might be thought of as an 'existence theorem': it is possible, not only in principle but also in practice, to pursue social justice in a global world. We know it is possible, because here is one way of doing it. Indeed, here are three: and there may be many more which may be even better. We might in any of those ways reasonably hope to globalize justice, at the same time as globalizing everything else.

Possibility is not certainty. Whether we succeed depends on how we play our cards, and on how others play theirs. Certainly we cannot expect to succeed instantly. My point is merely that there is no need to despair. There is room for moral manoeuvre, even within a hyperglobalized world – and all the more, of course, in the less-than-fully-globalized world that I think we actually inhabit.

Conclusion

In closing, let me recall an early petition against globalization of a rather different sort. The French satirist Bastiat, writing in 1846,

has the 'manufacturers of candles, tapers, lanterns, etc.' appealing
to the French Chamber of Deputies for relief, complaining:

> We are suffering from the ruinous competition of a foreign rival
> who apparently works under conditions so far superior to our own
> for the production of light that he is *flooding* the *domestic market*
> with it, at an incredibly low price . . . [T]he moment he appears,
> our sales cease, all the consumers turn to him, and a branch of
> French industry . . . is all at once reduced to complete stagnation.
> This rival . . . is none other than the sun . . .
>
> We ask you to be so good as to pass a law requiring the closing
> of all windows, dormers, skylights, inside and outside shutters,
> curtains, casements . . . in short, all openings . . . through which the
> light of the sun is wont to enter houses, to the detriment of [our]
> fair industries . . .[34]

If theorists of globalization are correct – and remember, I have
queried to what extent they are – then it would be just as pointless to appeal for a return to the days of trade preferences and
currency controls. The world in which nations are economically
autonomous, and hence have a free hand to pursue social policies
completely of their own choosing, is gone forever.

If hyperglobalizationists are right in that, then it is a sad day
indeed for social justice. All of our hard-won gains at home will
thus be undone. But campaigners for social justice should take
heart.

- As a matter of moral *principle*, principles of justice are properly
  seen as being *global in scope*.
- As a matter of political *practice*, globalizing justice through
  any of the three mechanisms I have been discussing should be
  seen as a *feasible ambition*.

Notes

I am grateful to audiences at the University of Bergen and the London
School of Economics for illuminating discussions of these issues.

Robert E. Goodin

1   World Bank, *World Development Report 1997: The State in a Changing World* (Washington DC: Oxford University Press for the World Bank, 1997).

2   Richard M. Titmuss, *The Gift Relationship* (London: Allen and Unwin, 1971). Some economists get the point, most do not. Compare James Tobin, 'On limiting the domain of inequality', *Journal of Law and Economics*, 13 (1970), pp. 263–78, with Kenneth J. Arrow, 'Gifts and exchanges', *Philosophy and Public Affairs*, 1 (1972), pp. 343–62, to which Peter Singer replies, *Philosophy and Public Affairs*, 2 (1973), pp. 312–20.

3   For evidence, see Alfred Pfaller, Ian Gough and Göran Therborn, *Can the Welfare State Compete? A Comparative Study of Five Advanced Capitalist Countries* (London: Macmillan, 1991); and David Held, Anthony McGrew, David Goldblatt and Jonathan Perraton, *Global Transformations* (Cambridge: Polity, 1999).

4   Robert E. Goodin, 'Political ideals and political practice', *British Journal of Political Science*, 25 (1995), pp. 37–56.

5   Robert E. Goodin (ed.), *The Theory of Institutional Design* (Cambridge: Cambridge University Press, 1996).

6   Ernest Gellner, *Reason and Culture: The Historic Role of Rationality and Rationalism* (Oxford: Blackwell, 1992).

7   Amartya Sen, *Freedom and Development* (Cambridge: Cambridge University Press, 2000); Martha C. Nussbaum, *Women and Human Development* (Cambridge: Cambridge University Press, 2000); World Bank, 'Index of indicators', in *World Development Indicators 2001*, at www.worldbank.org/data/wdi2001/pdfs/index.pdf (accessed 22 Dec. 2001).

8   John Rawls, *A Theory of Justice* (Cambridge, Mass.: Harvard University Press, 1971), pp. 90–5; cf. John Rawls, *Political Liberalism* (New York: Columbia University Press, 1993), lecture 5.

9   Henry Shue, *Basic Rights* (Princeton: Princeton University Press, 1980).

10 Alexander Passerin D'Entrèves, *Natural Law* (London: Hutchinson, 1970).

11 At least most people were inclined to think that way until the mad aftermath of September 11th: of which the less said the better.

12 Michael Walzer, *Spheres of Justice* (Oxford: Martin Robertson, 1983), ch. 2; David Miller, *On Nationality* (Oxford: Clarendon

Press, 1995); Henry Sidgwick, *The Methods of Ethics*, 7th edn (London: Macmillan, 1907).

13 William Godwin, *Enquiry Concerning Political Justice* (1793), book 2, ch. 2.

14 This is an argument that I have pursued at length elsewhere, in 'What is so special about our fellow countrymen?', *Ethics*, 98 (1988), pp. 663–86 and, with Philip Pettit, 'The possibility of special duties', *Canadian Journal of Philosophy*, 16 (1986), pp. 651–76.

15 Hugo Grotius, *The Law of War and Peace* (1625), book 2, ch. 2, sec. 16. See further Christian Wolff, *The Law of Nations Treated According to a Scientific Method* (1749), secs 147–50.

16 Robert E. Goodin, 'Justice in one jurisdiction, no more', *Philosophical Topics* (2003), forthcoming.

17 John Maynard Keynes, 'National self-sufficiency' (1933), in *Collected Writings*, ed. Donald Moggeridge (London: Macmillan, 1982), vol. 21, pp. 233–46. See similarly James Meade, 'The exchange policy of a socialist government' (1934), in *Collected Papers*, ed. Susan Howson (London: Unwin Hyman, 1988), vol. 3, pp. 11–26.

18 John Braithwaite and Peter Drahos, *Global Business Regulation* (Cambridge: Cambridge University Press, 2000), ch. 11.

19 Stephan Leibfried and Paul Pierson, 'Prospects for social Europe', *Politics and Society*, 20 (1992), pp. 333–66.

20 Sidney Tarrow, 'Transnational politics: contention and institutions in international politics', *Annual Review of Political Science*, 4 (2001), pp. 1–20; Margaret Keck and Kathryn Sikkink, *Activists beyond Borders: Advocacy Networks in International Politics* (Ithaca: Cornell University Press, 1998).

21 Thomas Risse, Stephen C. Ropp and Kathryn Sikkink (eds), *The Power of Human Rights: International Norms and Domestic Change* (Cambridge: Cambridge University Press, 1999).

22 Braithwaite and Drahos, *Global Business Regulation*, ch. 23.

23 Ibid., p. 277.

24 Ibid., p. 184.

25 Charles Lipson, 'Why are some international agreements informal?', *International Organization*, 45 (1991), pp. 495–538.

26 Thomas W. Pogge, *Realizing Rawls* (Ithaca: Cornell University Press, 1989).

27 John Locke, *Second Treatise on Government* (1690), para. 25.

28   Jean-Jacques Rousseau, *Discourse on the Origin of Inequality* (1755), part 2, para. 1.
29   Thomas M. Franck, *Fairness in International Law and Institutions* (Oxford: Clarendon Press, 1995), pp. 399–405, 430–4.
30   James Tobin, 'A proposal for international monetary reform', *Eastern Economic Journal*, nos 3–4 (July–Oct. 1978); Barry Eichengreen, James Tobin and Charles Wyplasz, 'Two cases for sand in the wheels of international finance', *Economic Journal*, 105 (1995), pp. 162–72; Mahbub ul Haq, Inge Kaul and Isabelle Grunberg (eds), *The Tobin Tax: Coping with Financial Volatility* (New York: Oxford University Press, 1996).
31   George F. Kennan, 'To prevent a world wasteland', *Foreign Affairs*, 48 (1970), pp. 401–13.
32   Montreal Protocol, 'Protocol on substances that deplete the ozone layer', *International Legal Materials*, 26 (1987), pp. 1550–61; Robert E. Goodin, 'International ethics and the environmental crisis', *Ethics and International Affairs*, 4 (1990), pp. 91–105.
33   Michael Taylor and Hugh Ward, 'Chickens, whales and lumpy public goods: alternative models of public-goods provision', *Political Studies*, 30 (1982), pp. 350–70.
34   Frédéric Bastiat, 'A petition' (1846), *Economic Sophisms*, trans. and ed. Arthur Goodard (Irvington-on-Hudson, N.Y.: Foundation for Economic Education, 1996), pp. 56–60.

4

Taking Embedded Liberalism Global: the Corporate Connection

John Gerard Ruggie

Twenty years ago I published a scholarly article that introduced the concept of embedded liberalism.[1] It told the story of how the capitalist countries learned to reconcile the efficiency of markets with the values of social community that markets themselves require in order to survive and thrive. That lesson did not come to them easily.

In the Victorian era, policy concern with the level of domestic employment and price stability was subordinated to maintaining the external value of currencies and, less consistently, to the strictures of free trade. But the growing democratization of national political life made that posture increasingly unsustainable, and the first so-called golden age of globalization unraveled. In the period between the two world wars the opposite was true: the unfettered quest for national policy autonomy – pushed by the political left, right and center alike – steadily undermined and ultimately destroyed an already fragile international economic order.

When a workable balance finally was struck it took on somewhat different forms in different countries, reflecting national political realities: in the US, the New Deal or Keynesian state, and in Europe social democracy or the social market economy. But the underlying idea was the same: a grand social bargain whereby all sectors of society agreed to open markets, which in some cases had become heavily administered if not autarchic in the 1930s, but also to contain and share the social adjustment costs that open markets inevitably produce. That was the essence of the embedded liberalism compromise: economic liberalization was embedded in social community.

Governments played a key role in enacting and sustaining this compromise: moderating the volatility of transaction flows across borders and providing social investments, safety nets and adjustment assistance – yet all the while pushing international liberalization. In the industrialized countries, this grand bargain formed the basis of the longest and most equitable economic expansion in human history.

So what is the problem today? For the industrialized countries, it is the fact that embedded liberalism presupposed an *international* world. It presupposed the existence of *national* economies, engaged in *external* transactions, conducted at *arm's length*, which governments could mediate at the *border* by tariffs and exchange rates, among other tools. The globalization of financial markets and production chains, however, challenges each of these premises and threatens to leave behind merely national social bargains.

The developing countries, of course, never enjoyed the privilege of cushioning the adverse domestic effects of market exposure in the first place. The majority lack the resources, institutional capacity, international support and, in some instances, the political interest on the part of their ruling elites. As a result, large parts of the developing world have been unable to exploit the opportunities offered by globalization for achieving poverty reduction and sustainable development.

Thus, "our challenge," United Nations Secretary-General Kofi Annan alerted the World Economic Forum in January 1999, ten months before the so-called Battle of Seattle, "is to devise a similar compact on the global scale, to underpin the new global economy. . . . Until we do," he predicted, "the global economy will be fragile and vulnerable – vulnerable to backlash from all the 'isms' of our post-cold-war world: protectionism, populism, nationalism, ethnic chauvinism, fanaticism and terrorism."[2]

Embedding the global market within shared social values and institutional practices represents a task of historic magnitude. The reason is obvious: there is no govern*ment* at the global level to act on behalf of the common good, as there is at the national level. And international institutions are far too weak to fully compensate. Accordingly, this chapter examines the role of certain social processes and movements in triggering the emergence of more inclusive forms of global govern*ance*. Specifically, I focus on the contribution of the dynamic interplay between civil society, business and the public sector over the issue of corporate social responsibility.

The chapter is divided into two main parts. First, I describe some of the main drivers of the anti-globalization backlash, especially the growing anxieties in the industrialized countries that the social embeddedness side of the equation is losing out to the dictates of globalization. Then I examine the evolution of voluntary initiatives involving civil society and the global business community to promote corporate social responsibility as one means of responding to the many challenges of globalization. In that context, I also summarize the key features of Annan's Global Compact, a UN initiative to engage the corporate community, in partnership with civil society and labor, to implement human rights, labor standards and environmental sustainability in its global domain. The burden of my argument, with due appreciation for the irony, is that the corporate sector, which has done more than any other to create the growing gaps between global economy and national communities, is being pulled into playing a key bridging role between them. In the process, a global public domain is emerging, which cannot substitute for effective action by states but may help produce it.

John Gerard Ruggie

The backlash

The globalization backlash has many sources, some better reasoned than others.[3] But three negative attributes of the recent era of global market integration stand out as having animated particular concern.

First, the benefits of globalization are distributed highly unequally. As the IMF's Managing Director, Horst Köhler, has conceded, "the disparities between the world's richest and poorest nations are wider than ever."[4] Large parts of the developing world are left behind entirely. Africa is less integrated into the global economy today than a decade ago, and insofar as it is, it is largely through commodity exports, which works to Africa's disadvantage as commodity prices have fallen steadily.

Moreover, apart from China, income disparities among the world's people, as distinguished from countries, either have not improved significantly during the past three decades or actually may have become worse, depending on how they are measured.[5] Much the same holds for global poverty rates. Even in the United States, the unprecedented boom of the 1990s barely budged the income shares of the bottom 20 percent of households, and then only briefly.[6]

There is no fully satisfactory or universally accepted explanation of the relationship between these disparities and globalization. But their coexistence over an extended period of time, coupled with excessive claims for globalization's beneficence by some of its most powerful advocates, themselves feed criticism and outright opposition, including by a growing number of mainstream economists.[7]

Second, the backlash is triggered by a growing imbalance in global rule making. Those rules that favor global market expansion have become more robust and enforceable in the last decade or two – intellectual property rights, for example, or trade dispute resolution through the World Trade Organization. But rules

96

intended to promote equally valid social objectives, be they labor standards, human rights, environmental quality or poverty reduction, lag behind and in some instances actually have become weaker.[8] One result is the situation where considerations of patent rights have trumped fundamental human rights and even pandemic threats to human life – at least until that clash became unbearable for the world's conscience over the HIV/AIDS treatment issue in Africa.[9]

Third, for many people globalization has come to mean greater vulnerability to unfamiliar and unpredictable forces that can bring on economic instability and social dislocation, sometimes at lightning speed. The Asian financial crisis of 1997–8 was such a force – the fourth but not the last major international financial crisis in just two decades. Indeed, the integrity of cultures and sovereignty of states increasingly are seen to be at risk. Even in the most powerful countries, people worry for their jobs, wonder who is in charge and fear that their voices are drowned out in globalization's wake.

The long struggle that ultimately resulted in the embedded liberalism compromise suggests that disparities of this sort are socially unsustainable. Unless they are attended to they are bound to trigger some of the "isms" of which Annan warned – disrupting and potentially undermining the open global economy. What is more, the backlash against globalization has particular bite because it is driven not only, or even primarily, by the poor and the weak. Its vanguard includes large numbers of people in the most privileged societies the world has ever known.

Therefore, let us look briefly at some of the issues that trigger people's anxieties about globalization in the industrialized countries, and how much staying power their concerns are likely to have. Much of the debate about whether globalization is adversely affecting the social embeddedness of market forces focuses on its impact on levels of public expenditure and on public policy, especially in areas related to social safety nets; wage and employment levels; and more elusive issues of identity and accountability.

Public expenditure

Vito Tanzi and Ludger Schuknecht document the evolution of public expenditure in the industrialized countries going back to 1870.[10] Over the course of the subsequent 125 years, spending grew from an average of 10.7 percent of gross domestic product, to 45.6 percent. The two world wars and the Great Depression accounted for significant increases. But the most dramatic expansion took place between 1960 and 1980, and in that period social expenditures – for education, health, pensions, unemployment benefits and the like – more than doubled on average. This was also the period of the most significant reductions in barriers to trade and monetary flows by the industrialized countries. Research by political scientists as long ago as the late 1970s demonstrated a relationship between the two: the most open economies also tended to lead in social spending.[11] Broadly speaking, this pattern was in keeping with the embedded liberalism compromise of providing a certain measure of domestic compensation for the risks attending greater international openness.[12]

The 1980s and 1990s saw the emergence of growing skepticism about the role of the state, especially in the United Kingdom and the United States. For a variety of reasons, some substantive, others political, prevailing economic theory and public attitudes began to shift in a neoliberal (the preferred term for neo-laissez-faire) direction.[13] Though public spending continued to increase, it was at a slower pace. And it was purchasing fewer social services, in part due to the declining cost-effectiveness of some interventions, and in part because a rapidly rising public sector debt burden consumed an ever greater fraction of overall government spending.[14] A period of reform and retrenchment ensued.[15]

Tanzi and Schuknecht predict a reduction in public expenditure relative to GDP in the years ahead, reflecting less favorable attitudes toward the role of the state (which may be partially off-set in the United States by the effects of 9/11 and corporate malfeasance), coupled with greater fiscal constraints due to demographic shifts, among other factors.

But what exactly is the relationship between these trends and globalization? An increasingly widespread view holds that global market integration induces governments to pursue greater fiscal austerity, ease regulatory and tax burdens on business, and strongly discourage certain policy options if not ruling them out altogether[16] – owing to the relative increase in capital mobility if nothing else.[17] Geoffrey Garrett has examined aspects of this relationship closely – and skeptically – for some time. In a book published in 1998, he argued that social democracy continued to thrive where powerful left-of-center parties were allied with strong and centralized trade unions – irrespective of differences in the extent of market integration.[18] In other words, domestic coalitional politics appeared to be a more powerful explanation of social spending and related policy outcomes than globalization.[19]

But in a recent and more comprehensive statistical analysis Garrett has modified some of his earlier conclusions in at least three key respects. He now finds that year-to-year increases in total trade *do* have a negative effect on government spending, even though historically a country's exposure to trade was an important determinant of fiscal expansion.[20] He shows that increased international financial openness produces a similar result. And he finds that over time the average mix of taxation in the OECD countries has become somewhat less progressive – that is, "more revenues have been raised by tax sources that target poorer people."[21] Foreign direct investment had no such effects.

The magnitude of these changes remains small and patterns of variation among countries, and across different market segments for the same country, are exceedingly complex. Nevertheless, they may signal a gradual shift in the political economy of industrialized countries, away from an earlier "compensatory" approach to managing the effects of increased openness, toward more of a "competitiveness" model. This would confirm that popular anxiety about globalization, though possibly exaggerated, is not without any basis in fact. Recent moves by the United States Congress to limit offshore corporate tax havens and to couple President Bush's "fast track" trade negotiation authority with assistance to adversely affected workers indicate that even America's lawmakers – seemingly inured to this issue for the past two decades – have begun to recognize its political salience.[22]

Income and employment

In the United States, organized labor has been among the most ardent opponents of globalization, especially of further trade liberalization. Although third party presidential candidate Ross Perot coined the phrase, labor's concern has been driven by fear of a "giant sucking sound" of well-paying jobs being exported to low-wage countries.

There is little dispute that median family income in the United States has been stagnant for two decades while worker productivity has been growing.[23] And there can be no disagreement that this gap coincides with large increases in trade exposure.

But there any consensus ends. Edward Leamer has developed a sophisticated economic model and presents country-based evidence partly supporting the globalization hypothesis.[24] In contrast, Robert Lawrence and Matthew Slaughter's statistical study leads them to conclude that "trade had nothing to do with the slow increase in average compensation," that low rates of productivity increases in the non-traded goods sector of the American economy have been responsible.[25] Paul Krugman, among others, has argued that technological change, especially information technology, is the main cause.[26]

Disentangling and establishing these and other factors with any degree of certainty, Leamer acknowledges, "may be inherently too complex for economists to handle."[27] Dani Rodrik suggests that the link between globalization and its labor market effects may be largely indirect, through shifts in relative bargaining power.[28] Globalization makes the services of large numbers of workers more

easily substitutable across national boundaries, Rodrik argues, as
a result of which the leverage of immobile labor vis-à-vis mobile
capital erodes. Thus, in the neoliberal countries workers are obliged
to accept greater instability in earnings and hours worked, if not
lower wages altogether; to pay a larger share of their own benefits (as has become all too evident in the area of pensions and
health care) as well as improvements in working conditions; and
to accept more frequent job changes. Along similar lines, Jagdish
Bhagwati uses the term "kaleidoscopic" rather than "flexible" to
describe the highly volatile US labor markets, thereby better
conveying the nervousness they induce.[29] In the more traditional
social democracies and social market economies where income
levels and employment are more secure, labor is obliged to accept
higher rates of chronic unemployment and lack of job creation.

Thus, the impact of globalization on wage stagnation in the US
and high unemployment in Europe remains at minimum an open
question for the economy as a whole. Of course, it is not an open
question for workers in the industries affected most directly by
job-displacing imports, who may have to accept lower-paying
work. And if domestic compensatory measures erode at the same
time, as discussed in the previous section, then labor's opposition
to globalization should hardly come as a surprise.

Identity and accountability

On the eve of the WTO's 1999 Seattle ministerial meeting, the
University of Maryland's Program on International Policy Attitudes published a study of Americans' attitudes toward trade, and
globalization more broadly.[30] A solid majority expressed support
for trade liberalization in principle. Only 30 percent felt it was
going too fast; the rest felt that it was proceeding at the right
speed (62 percent) or too slowly (23 percent).

But in practice business was seen to be the prime beneficiary:
61 percent of respondents felt that business was better off as
a result of lower barriers, compared to only 25 percent who

believed workers were. Overwhelming majorities felt that US trade policy-makers were giving "too little" consideration to "working Americans" (72 percent), "the general public" (68 percent) or "people like you" (73 percent). Furthermore, 60 percent felt that policy-makers paid too little attention to trade's "impact on the environment."

However, overall support for trade liberalization soared (to 84 percent) when respondents were offered the option that the government would help workers adapt to changes associated with increased trade. Moreover, 78 percent felt that the WTO should consider issues like labor standards and the environment when it makes trade decisions; and respondents were fully prepared to support trade sanctions to advance these (and related) social goals. As for globalization – conceived as the broader process of growing interconnectedness in the world – respondents saw it as having a mixture of positive and negative elements, with the positives moderately outweighing the negatives.

In short, the Maryland study makes it clear that the American public is far from being protectionist. But it views the benefits of open trade to be unequally distributed, and safeguards for workers, labor standards and the environment to be inadequate.

In a recent survey of Canadian public attitudes Matthew Mendelsohn and Robert Wolfe further differentiate attitudes toward trade liberalization from attitudes toward globalization. And they conduct a causal analysis relating those attitudes to relevant attributes of the respondents.[31]

Mendelsohn and Wolfe find that Canadians strongly support new trade agreements (65 percent positive responses), including a Free Trade Area of the Americas (67 percent positive). But they are dubious about encouraging more rapid globalization (only 45 percent positive). Moreover, while respondents strongly favored international cooperation and policy coordination – as is typical of Canadians' attitudes – they fundamentally opposed ceding national control over labor and workplace standards (a mere

27 percent positive) or standards for social programs (just 17 percent) – consequences they closely associate with globalization.

The causal chains behind these differences are even more striking.[32] The authors find that Canadians' attitudes toward trade reflect individuals' calculations of self-interest as economic agents – their level of education or skill, for example, and thus their sense of personal competitiveness in the global marketplace. But interest-based factors fail utterly to account for views about globalization. So whereas education, for example, is strongly related to attitudes toward trade, it is irrelevant to how the respondents feel about globalization. Instead, responses to globalization reflect Canadians' sense of identity as citizens and their core values concerning the kind of society in which they wish to live – and the respondents viewed the Canadian welfare state as a core feature of both.

If this is true in Canada it is bound to be all the more so within European Union countries, where identity politics is doubly jolted by globalization and political integration – the latter itself being, in part, a response to globalization.

To sum up, the industrialized countries appear to have passed through the 1990s with a fraying of domestic social safety nets, though not a dismantling. But the trend lines have been heading in negative directions. Moreover, anxieties about globalization appear to reflect individuals' fears not only about potential economic risks and losses, but also about losses measured in terms of identity and control. Unless these doubts about globalization are countered, therefore, they can only be expected to grow.

But, as we shall now see, those same anxieties about globalization also have helped generate and sustain civil society initiatives aimed at managing the adverse effects of globalization more directly, without waiting for states or international organizations to get around to acting. I now turn to that subject, beginning with a brief sketch of the expanding role of civil society in global governance.

John Gerard Ruggie

Voluntary initiatives

Once upon a time, governance at the international level was entirely a statist affair. Whether the instruments were international alliances, regimes, law and organizations, or transnational networks of national bureaucracies, states both monopolized the conduct of governance and were the primary objects of their joint decisions and actions. That was the foundational premise of the traditional system.

In recent decades, actors and forces for which the territorial state is not the cardinal organizing principle have begun to outflank the state externally and to gnaw away at its governance monopoly from the inside. They may be driven by universal values or factional greed, by profit and efficiency considerations or the search for salvation. They include global financial markets and production chains, civil society organizations and such uncivil entities as transnational terrorist and criminal networks.

The place of non-state actors and movements remains poorly understood in the mainstream literature, largely because they tend to be viewed, implicitly if not explicitly, through the lenses of an "institutional substitutability" premise.[33] That is to say, if other institutional forms at the international level do not have the potential to *replace* the territorial state they tend to be regarded as unworthy of serious consideration: interesting in practice, perhaps, but not in theory. And the fact is that the state is not disappearing, even in the increasingly integrated European Union.[34]

Nevertheless, significant institutional developments *are* evolving at the global level, among them the emergence of what we might call a global public domain: an arena of discourse, contestation and action organized around global rule making – a transnational space that is not exclusively inhabited by states, and which permits the direct expression and pursuit of human interests, not merely those mediated by the state.[35] One of its major drivers is the expanding role of civil society, and the interplay between civil society organizations and the global corporate sector.[36] This institutional development does not and cannot take the place of states, but it introduces new elements and new dynamics into the processes of global governance.

Civil society organizations

Real world players have come to recognize the involvement of civil society organizations (CSOs) in several areas related to global rule making – where by "recognize" I mean that the other players regard CSOs' participation as more or less legitimate, and in varying degrees they actually count on them to play those roles.[37] In other words, the roles have become institutionalized – much as, for example, the environmental movement did within the industrialized countries a generation ago.[38]

To begin with, civil society organizations have become the main international providers of direct assistance to people in developing countries, be it foreign aid, humanitarian relief or a variety of other internationally provided services. Governmental entities, such as the United States Agency for International Development, largely have become contracting agencies while CSOs deliver the goods.

In a normative vein, CSOs play increasingly important roles in generating, deepening and implementing transnational norms in such areas as human rights, the environment and anti-corruption. They do so through their own global campaign activities, but also by direct involvement in official governance forums like the UN's human rights machinery, where the documentation provided by Amnesty International, for example, carries weight precisely because it is detached from any national interest.[39]

CSO coalitions also have become a significant, if still episodic, force in blocking or promoting international agreements. Two exemplars have acquired iconic status. The most celebrated blockage was of the Multilateral Agreement on Investment (MAI), negotiated at the Organization for Economic Cooperation and Development (OECD), which would have been the high water mark of the neoliberal quest in the 1990s.[40] And the most dramatic instance of successfully promoting a new agreement – even participating fully in its negotiation – is the land-mines ban, which was begun, literally, by two people with a fax machine, and ended up helping to produce an international treaty over the opposition of the most powerful bureaucracy in the world's most powerful state: the US Pentagon.[41] More conventional CSO lobbying contributed to the creation of the International Criminal Court. CSOs also are a powerful source of political pressure for reforming international organizations, especially the Bretton Woods institutions and the WTO.[42]

Coalitions of domestic and transnational civil society networks also perform indispensable roles in the defense of human and labor rights, environmental standards and other social concerns within countries where the normal political process impedes or opposes progress in those areas. A key mechanism is the so-called boomerang effect, first identified by Keck and Sikkink, whereby domestic civil society actors link up with international actors, including other CSOs, states and international organizations, to bring external pressure to bear on the target state(s).[43]

Finally, civil society organizations have become a major force to induce greater social responsibility in the global corporate sector, by creating transparency in the overseas behavior of companies and their suppliers and creating links to consumers back home.[44] The last of these is of greatest interest for the purposes of the present chapter.

Corporate social responsibility

The rights enjoyed by transnational corporations have increased manyfold over the past two decades, as a result of multilateral trade agreements, bilateral investment pacts and domestic liberalization. Along with those rights, however, have come demands, led largely by civil society, that corporations accept commensurate obligations. To oversimplify only slightly, as governments were creating the space for transnational corporations (TNCs) to operate globally, other social actors have sought to infuse that space with greater corporate social responsibility.

Civil society organizations have joined issue with the global corporate sector for several reasons. First, individual companies have made themselves targets by doing "bad" things in the past: Shell in Nigeria, Nike in Indonesia, Nestlé in relation to its breast milk substitute products, unsafe practices in the chemical industry as symbolized by Union Carbide's Bhopal disaster, upscale apparel retailers purchasing from sweatshop suppliers, unsustainable forestry practices by the timber industry, and so on. Even where companies may be breaking no laws, they have been targeted by activist groups for violating the companies' own self-proclaimed standards or broader community norms in such areas as human rights, labor practices and environmental sustainability. CSOs seek to induce companies to undertake verifiable change.

Second, the growing imbalance between corporate rights and obligations itself has become a major factor driving CSO campaigns and, as I suggested earlier, it has particular resonance where it touches on life-and-death issues like HIV/AIDS treatment and related public health crises. In that particular instance, the pharmaceutical industry's pricing policy, combined with its insistence on protecting patent rights, prevented access to treatment for millions of poor people in poor countries. Civil society successfully framed price reductions as a corporate obligation.

Gradually, however, the sheer fact that the corporate sector, unlike states and international organizations, has global reach and capacity has become its most compelling attraction to other social actors, together with its ability to make and implement decisions at a pace that neither governments nor intergovernmental agencies can possibly match. In the face of global governance gaps and governance failures, civil society – and increasingly other actors as well, including states – seeks to engage the corporate world's global platform to advance broader social objectives. Kofi Annan's Global Compact, discussed below, is based entirely on this rationale.

The universe of transnational corporations consists roughly of 63,000 firms, with more than 800,000 subsidiaries and millions of suppliers.[45] Improving those companies' social and environmental performance has direct benefits for their employees and the communities in which they operate. But equally important is the potential for generating positive social spillover effects. In the developing world, the adoption of good practices by major firms may exert an upward pull on the performance of local enterprises in the same sector.[46] And in the industrialized countries, the gradual diffusion of good practices by major companies' social and environmental performance abroad may lessen the fear that a global "race to the bottom" will undermine their own policy frameworks for achieving social inclusion and economic security at home.

In sum, as a result of pressure from civil society, companies and business associations began to accept, on a voluntary basis and at a modest pace, new corporate social responsibilities in their own corporate domains, and more recently vis-à-vis society at large. The decision by firms to engage is driven by a variety of factors, but above all by the sensitivity of their corporate brands to consumer attitudes.

Certification institutions

Transnational corporations have adopted scores of codes of conduct and negotiated others within industry associations and with CSOs. Gary Gereffi and his colleagues call these "certification institutions."[47] By now they exist in most major economic sectors, including mining, petroleum, chemicals, forest products, automobiles as well as textiles, apparel and footwear. A recent OECD survey inventoried 246 codes, though the total number remains unknown.[48] In that survey, labor standards (heavy concentration in the apparel industry) and environmental concerns (high in the extractive sector) dominate other issues addressed (148 and 145 cases respectively), with some codes including both.

The initial wave consisted largely of unilateral company codes. They made it possible for firms to claim that their behavior was governed by a code of conduct, but without, for the most part, sharing its details with the public. Of the 118 companies with individual codes included in the OECD survey, for example, only 24 indicated any form of public disclosure of company compliance.[49] And company codes are far more likely to address practices found objectionable by industrialized country consumers than possibly more pervasive problems that entail fewer reputational risks – in the area of labor standards, for instance, workplace harassment and child labor dominate, with freedom of association trailing well behind.

Individual exceptions have always existed, such as Levi Strauss, which pioneered a transparent worldwide code for manufacturing and contractors as long ago as 1991.[50] In 2002, the Royal Dutch/ Shell group became the first company to combine its social and financial reports into one, believing that investors should see the full picture of the company's performance.[51] In the interval, some branded apparel retailers began to audit supplier compliance with company codes, in many cases using respected third-party instruments like SA8000.[52] Two major standardized systems for reporting companies' social and environmental performance are now on-stream as well, AccountAbility1000 and the Global Reporting Initiative.[53]

Other companies are learning that talk is not cheap. Nike, for example, is in the California courts under that state's Unfair Business Practices Act, accused of making misrepresentations, false statements and material omissions in literature about working conditions in its supply chain in an attempt to maintain or increase sales. The California Superior Court ruled that Nike's promotional statements were not protected as free speech but constituted commercial speech, and it allowed an individual consumer's suit against the company to go forward.[54]

The most ambitious and typically the most transparent certification arrangements tend to be sectoral in scope, and to involve

several companies and/or business associations along with civil
society participants. Their aims range from ensuring that the price
paid to cooperatives of small-scale family farmers growing coffee
beans in Costa Rica includes a premium for growing the beans
in an environmentally sustainable manner (Fair Trade Certified
coffee); to ensuring that plywood ending up at Home Depot and
other participating home improvement outlets is produced in accordance with sustainable forestry practices (Forest Stewardship
Council); to certifying that sweatshirts sold in college bookstores
or cashmere sweaters destined for Fifth Avenue department stores
and upscale suburban malls are knitted in conditions that meet
agreed labor standards and conditions (Workers Rights Consortium, and either the Fair Labor Association or an individual company code with compliance audited by SA8000). A certification
institution called Responsible Care – triggered by Bhopal – now
operates in the US chemical industry, while the Global Mining
Initiative was recently launched in that sector.

Many such arrangements now exist – there are 22 additional
certification institutions in the forest products industry alone, for
instance, and the US-based Workers Rights Consortium is closely
coordinated with European initiatives like the Clean Clothes
Campaign.[55] Their rate of increase over the past decade has been
extraordinary.

The Global Compact

Kofi Annan coupled his 1999 warning to the world's business
leaders about the fragility of globalization with an initiative called
the Global Compact (GC). It is *not* a code of conduct – which has
been a major point of contention vis-à-vis anti-globalization activist groups.[56] A partnership between the United Nations, business,
international labor and major transnational civil society organizations, the Compact instead seeks to engage companies in the promotion of certain UN principles within corporate domains.[57] The
principles themselves are drawn from the Universal Declaration of

Human Rights, the International Labor Organization's Fundamental Principles on Rights at Work and the Rio Principles on Environment and Development.[58] Companies are encouraged to move toward "good practices" as defined through multi-stakeholder dialogue and partnership, rather than relying on their often superior bargaining position vis-à-vis national authorities, especially in small and poor states, to get away with less. The Compact employs three instruments to achieve its aims.

Through its "learning forum," it is designed to generate consensus-based understandings of how a company's commitment to the nine principles can be translated most effectively into corporate management practices. The idea is for the UN to publicize these norms, thereby providing a standard of comparison for – and adding public pressure on – industry laggards. The learning forum is still in its infancy and so its performance cannot yet be assessed.

By means of its "policy dialogues," the Compact generates shared understandings about, for example, the socially responsible posture for companies when operating in countries afflicted by conflict. This particular dialogue has explored how companies can conduct impact assessments and reduce the risks that their own behavior may fuel such conflicts; achieve greater transparency in their financial transactions with the parties to conflicts; and devise revenue sharing regimes that will benefit local populations.[59] The results from these dialogues play a normative role in the broader public arena, and they directly inform the UN's own conflict prevention and peacemaking activities.

Finally, through its "partnership projects" in developing countries the Compact contributes to capacity building where it is needed most. Ongoing cases include support for microlending, investment promotion, HIV/AIDS awareness programs for employees in sub-Saharan Africa, devising sustainable alternatives to child labor, and a host of initiatives in ecoefficiency and other dimensions of environmental management. One of the success stories at the Johannesburg World Summit on Sustainable

Development was the Global Compact partnership effort to promote investment in the least developed countries.[60]

Companies initiate participation in the Compact with a letter of commitment from their Chief Executive Officer to the Secretary-General, a step that often requires board approval. Since a kickoff event in July 2000, some 400 companies worldwide – based in Europe, the United States, Japan, Hong Kong, India, Brazil, Thailand and elsewhere – have done so.[61]

Organizationally, the Compact comprises a series of nested networks. The Secretary-General's office provides strategic direction, policy coherence and quality control. The participating UN agencies, companies, international labor, transnational NGOs, and university-based research centers do the heavy lifting in the learning forum, policy dialogues and partnership projects.

The Global Compact has triggered several complementary regional, national, and sectoral initiatives. Typically, they take a subset of interested GC participants beyond its minimum commitments. For example, Norway's Statoil and the International Federation of Chemical, Energy, Mine and General Workers' Unions reached an agreement within the GC framework whereby Statoil is extending the same labor rights as well as health and safety standards to all its overseas operations that it applies in Norway – including in Vietnam, Venezuela, Angola, and Azerbaijan.[62] A Nordic Global Compact Network has been established, as has a "Friends of the Global Compact" network in Germany, both pursuing additional work programs of interest to their participants. Pilot projects for country-level counterparts – "local compacts" – are under way in some 20 developing countries, under the leadership of the United Nations Development Program. In addition, a number of initiatives intended for other purposes have associated themselves with the GC. The most unusual is the multi-stakeholder Committee for Melbourne, which incorporated the GC principles into the strategic plan it developed for that Australian city (City Plan 2010), and is encouraging all firms doing business there to embrace them.[63]

As noted, the Compact is not a code of conduct but a social learning network.[64] It operates on the premise that socially legitimated good practices will help drive out bad ones through the power of transparency and competition. The UN General Assembly could not generate a meaningful code of conduct at this time even if that were deemed desirable; the only countries that would be eager to launch such an effort are equally unfriendly to the private sector, human rights, labor standards and the environment.[65] In any event, many of the GC's principles cannot be defined at this time with the precision required for a viable intergovernmental code. No consensus exists on precisely what comprises a "precautionary approach" – that in the face of environmental uncertainty the bias should favor avoiding risk – even though the principle was enshrined at the 1992 Rio Conference. Similarly, no consensus exists, even among advocates, on where, in long and complex chains of relationships, to set the threshold of corporate "complicity" in human rights abuses.[66] Accumulated experience – through trial, error and social vetting – will gradually fill in the blanks.

Moreover, ex ante standards often become performance ceilings that are difficult to change – witness the inability of the US Senate to muster the political will to improve automobile fuel efficiency standards that have not been altered since 1985, long before the prevalence of so-called sports utility vehicles.[67] In contrast, the Compact seeks to peg company performance globally to evolving international community-based "good practices," thereby potentially "ratcheting up" performance on an ongoing basis.[68]

The Global Compact is based on principles that were universally endorsed by governments, thus stipulating aspirational goals of the entire international community. It enlists partners in the corporate sector and civil society to help bridge the gap between aspiration and reality – to become agencies for the promotion of community norms. Thus, the Compact is a heterodox addition to the growing menu of responses to globalization's challenges that engage the private sector – including corporate codes of conduct, social and environmental reporting initiatives, and various other means to promote and monitor corporate social responsibility.

A global public domain

Despite the great progress that has been achieved in promoting voluntary initiatives, their scope remains limited. For example, the Forest Stewardship Council (FSC) has certified 70 million acres of forests, which amounts to a mere 4 percent of the total acreage controlled by timber companies.[69] Similarly, sales of Fair Trade Certified coffee are estimated to have been 30 million pounds in 2001, a tiny fraction of total global coffee sales.[70] Fewer than 200 firms out of a total of 1,500 participate in the US chemical industry's Responsible Care program.[71] Of the 700 companies subscribing to the Global Compact, perhaps no more than a quarter are deeply engaged. And so on, throughout other industry sectors. By themselves, therefore, they do not and cannot constitute the entirety of solutions.

At the same time, these company-based initiatives are significant not only for what they achieve directly, but also because they are triggering broader second-order consequences. Consider some of the main elements and actors.

First, the investment community has shown growing interest, which brings large amounts of capital into play. Instruments for socially responsible investment, like the Domini and Calvert mutual funds, are proliferating, and major pensions funds, including America's largest, the California Public Employee Retirement System, have made socially responsible investment a priority.[72]

Second, the public sector is slowly entering the picture. Several OECD countries – the UK, France and the Netherlands – have begun to encourage or require companies to engage in social reporting, for example, and to promote corporate social responsibility through other means; the European Union has issued a green paper on the subject.[73] And the 2002 World Summit on Sustainable Development would have been an outright failure were it not for the many public–private partnership projects it generated.[74] Some governments entered these in part to avoid more binding commitments, to be sure, including the United States, which sought to avoid any targets or timetables; but they also look to such partnerships as a means to leverage limited resources, and to learn by doing in the face of high risk and uncertainty.[75]

Where labor is included in voluntary initiatives – as in the Global Compact – it gains a global platform that may help compensate for, and possibly overcome, its stagnant and even shrinking platform at the national level. Indeed, no social partner has made more effective use of the Global Compact than labor.

Perhaps the most significant development politically is the emergence of a new advocate for a more effective global public sector: business itself. Corporate leaders at the frontier of corporate social responsibility issues have begun to realize that the concept is infinitely elastic: the more they do, the more they will be asked to do. As a result, business leaders themselves have begun to ask, "*Where* is the public sector?" Three elite global business groups – the World Economic Forum, International Chamber of Commerce, and World Business Council for Sustainable Development – recently launched governance initiatives, not to *curtail* the public sector but to clarify where private sector responsibility ends and public responsibility begins.[76]

Similarly, in the staggering HIV/AIDS treatment crisis in Africa, as the major pharmaceutical companies have been forced to lower their prices, and as employers such as Anglo American Mines have been obliged to begin gratis treatment programs for their employees – a third of whom are infected in Anglo's case – they have become strong advocates for public sector capacity building in education and public health alike.[77]

Finally, at the end of the day the accumulation of experience inevitably will lead to a desire for greater benchmarking, for moving from "good" to "best" practices and even formal codification, so that some of the "soft law" products of voluntary initiatives are likely to become "harder" law down the road. The advocates will include industry leaders to lock in their own first-mover advantages, or wanting a level playing field vis-à-vis laggards – as happened when several major energy companies lobbied the US Congress for some form of greenhouse-gas limits after President Bush rejected the Kyoto Protocol.[78] Laggards have a harder time opposing standards based on actual achievements by their peers than ex ante standards.

This terrain is fraught with strategic manipulation and the potential for shirking. But it also opens the door to more firmly institutionalizing an emerging global public domain by bringing the public sector into it. Globalization was a one-way bet for the business community: governments were needed to create the space within which business could expand and integrate, but they were not otherwise welcome. The combination of global governance gaps and governance failures, however, created an organizational niche that civil society actors began to occupy, and from which they have been engaging the global business community in the attempt to balance its newly acquired rights with new social responsibilities. Now we are slowly beginning to come full circle: business wants help to channel some of the pressure it faces into the construction of at least minimally effective public sectors, including at the global level. This sets up the possibility of a very different political dynamic than existed as recently as the 1990s.

Conclusion

When we reflect on how hard it was and how long it took to institute the original embedded liberalism compromise at the national level, the prospect of achieving a similar social framing of global market forces seems exponentially more daunting. But if there is one similarity between the two eras, and the two levels of social organization, it is in the respective roles of the private sector as an inadvertent transformational force – be it the hegemony of the great "trusts" in the late nineteenth century, the abysmal failure of financial institutions in the interwar period, or the spread of multinational corporate empires today. The international political arena differs radically, characterized as it is by the absence of government. And so at the global level there will be many more zigs, many more zags, and quite probably many more failures. But our discussion has outlined both a dynamic of possible change and a possible trajectory.

I have argued that, as a result of the expansion of civil society and its engagement with the corporate sector, a global public domain is emerging. I take that to mean an arena inhabited by various actors for whom the territorial state is not the cardinal organizing principle, as well as by states; and wherein a variety of human interests are expressed and pursued directly, not merely those mediated – promoted, filtered, interpreted – by the state. Indeed, some areas of global public policy would barely exist were it not for non-state actors. And in addition to the traditional machinery of interstate governance, the likes of essentially private certification institutions are becoming significant components of global rule making. But private governance produces only partial solutions, and its own unfolding brings the public sector back in.

It is difficult at this early stage to be more precise, and thus it is doubly imperative not to exaggerate either the virtues or the defects of these institutional developments. In view of the fragility of voluntary initiatives like certification institutions and the Global Compact, it seems highly implausible to depict them as expressions of the rise of global "corporatism," for example, let alone conjuring up the ghost of corporatism's fascist ancestry as a scenario for the global future.[79] At the same time, it also seems at least premature to view them as expressions of cosmopolitan democracy.[80] Greater pluralism, perhaps; but we are a long way from turning rich country consumers, the employees of transnational corporations or even dedicated activists into global citizens. Moreover, the skewed distribution of agential capacity between North and South is too pronounced, accountability problems too

117

pervasive and the distributional consequences of these kinds of global governance instruments too poorly understood for us to believe that they reflect some new stable equilibrium.

What we can say is that a fundamental recalibration is going on of the public–private sector balance, and it is occurring at the global level no less than the domestic. Haltingly and erratically, something akin to an embedded liberalism compromise is being pulled and pushed into the global arena, and the corporate connection is a key element in that process.

Notes

Earlier versions of this chapter were presented as the keynote address at the conference on Global Governance: Towards a New Grand Compromise? at the University of Toronto, May 29, 2002; a Miliband Public Lecture on Global Economic Governance, London School of Economics and Political Science, June 6, 2002; and the keynote paper for the theme panel on International Relations Theory and Global Governance, American Political Science Association, Annual Meeting, Boston, Aug. 31, 2002. I am most grateful to participants at each event for their probing questions and constructive comments.

1 John Gerard Ruggie, "International Regimes, Transactions and Change: Embedded Liberalism in the Postwar Economic Order," *International Organization*, 36 (Spring 1982). The essay drew on Karl Polanyi's classic and still unsurpassed account of these wrenching struggles in *The Great Transformation* (Boston: Beacon Press, 1944); for a recent economic history see Harold James, *The End of Globalization: Lessons from the Great Depression* (Cambridge, Mass.: Harvard University Press, 2001).

2 Kofi Annan, "A Compact for the New Century," Jan. 31, 1999 (UN, SG/SM/6881).

3 For a cross section of critiques see Robin Broad (ed.), *Global Backlash: Citizen Initiatives for a Just World Economy* (Lanham, Md.: Rowman and Littlefield, 2002). Also see the excellent analysis by Susan Ariel Aaronson, *Taking Trade to the Streets* (Ann Arbor: University of Michigan Press, 2001).

4   "Working for a Better Globalization," remarks by Horst Köhler at the Conference on Humanizing the Global Economy, Washington DC, Jan. 28, 2002.

5   The difficulties of statistical measurement are formidable. Robert Wade's chapter in this volume addresses the methodological issues and substantive findings, and reaches a pessimistic conclusion; also see Branko Milanovic, "The Two Faces of Globalization: Against Globalization As We Know It," available at www.worldbank.org/research/inequality/pdf/naiveglobl.pdf. On the other side, see Xavier Sala-i-Martin, "The Disturbing 'Rise' of Global Income Inequality," National Bureau of Economic Research Working Paper no. 8904, Apr. 2002.

6   The Census Bureau reports that the share of total household income accounted for by the bottom quintile increased to 3.7% in 1995, from 3.6% in 1993, but by 1997 it had dropped again to its earlier level, where it remained as of 2000. Carmen DeNavas-Walt, Robert W. Cleveland and Marc I. Roemer, *Money Income in the United States: 2000* (Washington DC: US Census Bureau, Sept. 2001), table C, p. 8. Current figures are noted in Louis Uchitelle, "Stagnant Wages Pose Added Risks to Weak Economy," *New York Times*, Aug. 11, 2002.

7   For example, Dani Rodrik has led the way in challenging World Bank claims that trade liberalization itself leads to greater success in promoting economic growth and poverty reduction, arguing that the causality and the sequencing are far more complex. Rodrik, "Comments on 'Trade, Growth, and Poverty,' by D. Dollar and A. Kraay," available at http://ksghome.harvard.edu~.drodrik.academic.ksg/Rodrik%20on%20Dollar-Kraay.PDF

8   For detailed surveys of what gets "regulated" at the global level, and how, see P. J. Simmons and Chantal de Jonge Oudraat (eds), *Managing Global Issues* (Washington DC: Carnegie Endowment, 2001), and John Braithwaite and Peter Drahos, *Global Business Regulation* (New York: Cambridge University Press, 2000).

9   The business community itself felt that the big pharmaceutical companies put themselves in an untenable position. Gardiner Harris and Laurie McGinley, "AIDS Gaffes in Africa Come Back to Haunt Drug Industry at Home," *Wall Street Journal*, Apr. 23, 2001.

10 Vito Tanzi and Ludger Schuknecht, *Public Spending in the 20th Century* (New York: Cambridge University Press, 2000).

John Gerard Ruggie

11 David R. Cameron, "The Expansion of the Public Economy: a Comparative Analysis," *American Political Science Review*, 72 (Dec. 1978); and Peter J. Katzenstein, "The Small European States in the International Economy," in John Gerard Ruggie (ed.), *The Antinomies of Interdependence* (New York: Columbia University Press, 1983).

12 Garrett seems to think that embedded liberalism should be measurable by some fixed formula linking year-to-year increases in the degree of openness to levels of growing social expenditure, allowing for a time lag. Geoffrey Garrett, "Capital Mobility, Exchange Rates and Fiscal Policy in the Global Economy," *Review of International Political Economy*, 7 (Spring 2000). But broad social frameworks of this sort work as constitutive expectations pertaining to an overall order of relations, not fixed bargains that govern every transaction. For a discussion of this difference in perspectives, see John Gerard Ruggie, "What Makes the World Hang Together? Neo-utilitarianism and the Social Constructivist Challenge," *International Organization*, 52 (Autumn 1998).

13 I concluded my 1982 article with the observation that the greatest threat to embedded liberalism came not from the so-called new protectionism, as was then widely assumed, "but the resurgent ethos of liberal capitalism" ("International Regimes, Transactions and Change," p. 413). Also see Mark Blyth, *Great Transformations: The Rise and Decline of Embedded Liberalism* (New York: Cambridge University Press, 2002).

14 Government expenditure on public debt rose rapidly from an average of 1.4% of GDP in 1970 to 4.5% in 1995. Tanzi and Schuknecht, *Public Spending in the 20th Century*, p. 46.

15 Mary Ruggie, *Realignments in the Welfare State* (New York: Columbia University Press, 1996).

16 Clearly financial market integration has increased the cost of utilizing capital controls. For example, when Malaysia imposed targeted and time-bound controls to limit domestic spillover from the Asian financial crisis, for which it had no responsibility, all the major credit rating agencies downgraded Malaysia's sovereign risk rating – Fitch IBCA to "junk bond" status. Said a spokesperson for Fitch: "We are in no doubt about Malaysia's ability to service its debt. It is a question of willingness to do so" – even though the Malaysian

government had done nothing to indicate any such unwillingness. See Rawi Abdelal and Laura Alfaro, "Malaysia: Capital and Control," Harvard Business School, Case 9-702-040 (June 4, 2002), p. 12.

17 Dani Rodrik, *Has Globalization Gone Too Far?* (Washington DC: Institute for International Economics, 1997).

18 Geoffrey Garrett, *Partisan Politics in the Global Economy* (New York: Cambridge University Press, 1998).

19 Of course, we would also want to know if globalization over time affects domestic coalitional possibilities. For one cut at this question see Jeffry A. Frieden and Ronald Rogowski, "The Impact of the International Economy on National Policies," in Robert O. Keohane and Helen V. Milner (eds), *Internationalization and Domestic Politics* (New York: Cambridge University Press, 1996).

20 Geoffrey Garrett and Deborah Mitchell, "Globalization, Government Spending and Taxation in the OECD," *European Journal of Political Research*, 39 (Mar. 2001), p. 147; and Garrett, "Capital Mobility, Exchange Rates and Fiscal Policy," p. 157. Interestingly, Garrett and Mitchell find no signs that this relationship is true specifically of trade with low-wage countries.

21 Garrett and Mitchell, "Globalization, Government Spending and Taxation," p. 159.

22 Congress agreed to spend up to $12 billion over a ten-year period for such assistance, including a tax credit for 65% of the cost of health insurance should workers lose their jobs to foreign competition. Congress also authorized a pilot project for wage insurance to dislocated workers, under which they would receive some compensation for lower wages in a new job. "Promoting the Noble Cause of Commerce," *The Economist*, Aug. 3, 2002.

23 See, for example, Richard B. Freeman and Lawrence Katz, "Rising Wage Inequality: The United States versus Other Advanced Countries," in Richard B. Freeman (ed.), *Working under Different Rules* (New York: Russell Sage Foundation, 1994).

24 Edward E. Leamer, "Wage Inequality from International Competition and Technological Change: Theory and Country Experience," American Economics Association, *Papers and Proceedings*, May 1996.

25 Robert Z. Lawrence and Matthew J. Slaughter, "International Trade and American Wages in the 1980s: Giant Sucking Sound or Small Hiccup?" *Brookings Papers on Economic Activity: Microeconomics*,

no. 2 (1993), citation on p. 165. One source of disagreement is that Lawrence and Slaughter find no evidence that labor-intensive tradable goods have declined in price (and thus driven down wages). Leamer suggests that a longer timespan must be considered because prices take time to ripple through the economy.

26 Paul Krugman, "Europe Jobless, America Penniless," *Foreign Policy*, 95 (Summer 1994); Paul Krugman and Robert Lawrence, "Trade, Jobs and Wages," *Scientific American*, 270 (April 1994); and Paul Krugman and A. J. Venables, "Globalization and the Inequality of Nations," *Quarterly Journal of Economics*, 110 (1995).

27 Leamer, "Wage Inequality," p. 311. Addressing specifically the effects of technological change, Leamer argues: "To do the job right, one really needs an accurate, complete, world-wide, long-run, general-equilibrium input-output model estimated from data that may or may not be available."

28 Rodrik, *Has Globalization Gone Too Far?*

29 Jagdish Bhagwati, "Trade and Wages: A Malign Relationship?" Columbia University, Department of Economics, Discussion Paper 761, Oct. 1995. Bhagwati's interpretation further stipulates that in such labor markets employers are reluctant to invest in training unskilled workers, putting them at a further disadvantage.

30 "Americans on Globalization," at http://pipa.org/OnlineReports/Globalization/global_rep.html.

31 Matthew Mendelsohn and Robert Wolfe, "Values, Interests and Globalization: The Continued Compromise of Embedded Liberalism," paper presented at the conference on Global Governance: Towards a New Grand Compromise? at the University of Toronto, May 29, 2002, available at http://qsilver.queensu.ca/~wolfer/General/research.html. Also see Mendelsohn and Wolfe, "Globalization, Trade Policy and the Permissive Consensus in Canada," *Canadian Public Policy*, 28, no. 3 (2002).

32 The regression results are reported in tables 3 and 4 of Mendelsohn and Wolfe, "Values, Interests and Globalization."

33 I first flagged this issue in John Gerard Ruggie, "Territoriality and Beyond: Problematizing Modernity in International Relations," *International Organization*, 46 (Winter 1993).

34 Of course, individual states on the periphery may fail as a result of collapsed internal authority and the usurpation of the state's

coercive apparatus for factional or private ends – as discussed in, for example, Mats Berdal and David M. Malone (eds), *Greed and Grievance: Economic Agendas in Civil Wars* (Boulder, Colo.: Lynne Rienner, 2000).

35   For good discussions of the concept of "public domain" – as distinct from, on the one side, the market and, on the other side, its narrower counterpart, the public sector – see Daniel Drache (ed.), *The Market or the Public Domain: Global Governance and the Asymmetry of Power* (London: Routledge, 2001).

36   I use the term "civil society organization" rather than NGO (non-governmental organization) to include transnational social movements, coalitions and activist campaigns as well as NGOs.

37   For useful introductions, see Sanjeev Khagram, James V. Riker and Kathryn Sikkink (eds), *Restructuring World Politics: Transnational Social Movements, Networks and Norms* (Minneapolis: University of Minnesota Press, 2002); Ann M. Florini (ed.), *The Third Force: The Rise of Transnational Civil Society* (Washington DC: Carnegie Endowment for International Peace, 2000); and Jessica Mathews, "Power Shift," *Foreign Affairs*, 76 (Jan./Feb. 1997).

38   A good comparable discussion may be found in Cary Coglianese, "Social Movements, Law, and Society: The Institutionalization of the Environmental Movement," *University of Pennsylvania Law Review*, 150 (Nov. 2001).

39   On human rights, see Thomas Risse, "The Power of Norms versus the Norms of Power: Transnational Civil Society and Human Rights," and on anti-corruption, Fredrik Galtung, "A Global Network to Curb Corruption: The Experience of Transparency International," in Florini, *The Third Force*.

40   A global coalition of CSOs made the case that certain of the MAI's provisions on investment protection would enable transnational corporations to challenge domestic environmental and labor standards on the grounds that they had the equivalent effect of expropriation, so that companies adversely affected could claim compensation. Supporting that fear was a 1996 case involving the Ethyl Corporation, which successfully sued the Canadian government under a similar provision of the North American Free Trade Agreement when Canada banned a gasoline additive Ethyl produced, with Canada agreeing to an out-of-court settlement of $13 million.

Andrew Walter, "NGOs, Business, and International Investment: The Multilateral Agreement on Investment, Seattle, and Beyond," *Global Governance*, 7 (Jan./Mar. 2001); and Stephen J. Kobrin, "The MAI and the Clash of Globalizations," *Foreign Policy*, 112 (Fall 1998). Both authors stress that factors other than activist pressure also contributed to the MAI's demise.

41 Motoko Mekata, "Building Partnerships toward a Common Goal: Experiences of the International Campaign to Ban Landmines," in Florini, *The Third Force*; and Ramesh Thakur and William Malley, "The Ottawa Convention on Landmines: A Landmark Humanitarian Treaty in Arms Control?" *Global Governance*, 5 (July/Sept. 1999).

42 Robert O'Brien, Jan Aart Scholte, Marc Williams and Anne Marie Goetz, *Contesting Global Governance* (New York: Cambridge University Press, 2000).

43 Margaret E. Keck and Kathryn Sikkink, *Activists beyond Borders* (Ithaca, N.Y.: Cornell University Press, 1998). Also see Daniel C. Thomas, *The Helsinki Effect: International Norms, Human Rights, and the Demise of Communism* (Princeton: Princeton University Press, 2001).

44 Good overviews may be found in Gary Gereffi, Ronie Garcia-Johnson and Erika Sasser, "The NGO-Industrial Complex," *Foreign Policy*, 125 (July/Aug. 2001), and several unpublished papers on their websites (www.env.duke.edu/solutions/colloquia-7th.html/, and www.env.duke.edu/solutions/research-envcert.html). On labor standards specifically, see Adelle Blackett, "Global Governance, Legal Pluralism and the Decentered State: A Labor Law Critique of Codes of Corporate Conduct," *Indiana Journal of Global Legal Studies*, 8 (2001), pp. 401–47.

45 The number of multinationals and their subsidiaries is reported in the *World Investment Report* (Geneva: United Nations Conference on Trade and Development, 2001). It is impossible to calculate the actual number of suppliers; Nike, for example, has approximately 750, and it is at the lower end among comparable firms in the number of factories as a fraction of its revenue base (personal communication from Nike executive).

46 Surprisingly little systematic research has been done on this question, in contrast to the volume of rhetoric it has generated. For a careful study in the environmental area, see Ronie Garcia-Johnson,

Exporting Environmentalism: US Multinational Chemical Corporations in Brazil and Mexico (Cambridge, Mass.: MIT Press, 2000).

47 See the sources in note 44.

48 OECD, Working Party of the Trade Committee, "Codes of Corporate Conduct – an Expanded Review of their Contents," TD/TC/WP(99)56/FINAL (June 7, 2000). Identifying the total universe of cases would require conducting a company-by-company survey, coupled with complementary surveys of industry associations and relevant CSOs – a prohibitive undertaking. Accordingly, the OECD warns that its inventory is neither a random nor a representative sample. In light of these data collection problems, much of the literature focuses on the far smaller but better known universe of sectoral multi-stakeholder codes and certification agreements; see Gereffi, Garcia-Johnson and Sasser, "The NGO-Industrial Complex."

49 "Codes of Corporate Conduct," table 6, p. 35.

50 www.levistrauss.com/responsibility.

51 www.shell.com/html/investor-en/shellreport01/reports2001/frameset.html.

52 SA8000, a system developed by Social Accountability International, covers a wide range of labor rights, health and safety standards, working conditions and compensation issues. It draws on the idea of quality control standards that are nearly universally used in the production of goods, and extends this concept to the treatment of workers. Companies subscribe to the SA8000 code or "management system," and their facilities are audited and "certified" by external auditors, who are themselves trained and certified by the SA8000 governing body. Deborah Leipziger, *SA8000: The Definitive Guide to the New Social Standard* (London: Financial Times/Prentice Hall, 2001).

53 Their attempt is to make social and environmental reporting as routine as financial reporting. Interestingly, the two systems reflect their respective national origins in their orientation: the GRI, a US invention, tries to capture the full range of possibilities by means of a large number of discrete indicators, whereas AA1000, which originated in the UK, is more concerned with instituting guiding principles and maximizing transparency. See www.globalreporting.org and www.accountability.org.uk.

54 Harriet Chiang, "Court says Nike must Defend its PR; Free Speech doesn't Protect Labor Claims," *San Francisco Chronicle*, May 3, 2002.

55 Erika N. Sasser, "Gaining Leverage: NGO Influence on Certification Institutions in the Forest Products Sector," paper presented at the 7th Annual Colloquium on Environmental Law and Institutions, Duke University, Dec. 7–8, 2001; and Blackett, "Global Governance, Legal Pluralism and the Decentered State."

56 Activist groups and some mainstream NGOs fear that because it is not a code of conduct, with explicit performance standards and compliance monitoring, the Compact gives companies a free ride. But as the following discussion tries to make clear, the Compact is a mechanism intended to engage companies in the promotion of UN goals, not to regulate them. Regulation is a perfectly valid objective, but it is not the only one that counts. The most vocal critic on this score is an anti-globalization group called CorpWatch, at www.corpwatch.org.

57 The GC participants include the UN (the Secretary-General's Office, Office of the High Commissioner for Human Rights, International Labor Organization, UN Environment Program and the UN Development Program); the International Confederation of Free Trade Unions (ICFTU); more than a dozen transnational NGOs in the three areas covered by the GC, such as Amnesty International, the International Union for the Conservation of Nature, and Oxfam; as well as individual companies and international business associations. For up-to-date information, see www.unglobalcompact.org.

58 The nine principles are: support and respect for the protection of internationally proclaimed human rights; non-complicity in human rights abuses; freedom of association and the effective recognition of the right to collective bargaining; the elimination of all forms of forced and compulsory labor; the effective abolition of child labor; the elimination of discrimination in respect of employment and occupation; a precautionary approach to environmental challenges; greater environmental responsibility; and encouragement of the development and diffusion of environmentally friendly technologies.

59 Consult www.unglobalcompact.org.

60 Ibid.

61 Brand vulnerability, as already indicated, is a key factor driving
companies headquartered in the industrialized countries. In addition, some companies in cutting edge industries have found that
they cannot sufficiently motivate the very best people with monetary rewards alone, as a result of which they have adopted more
elevated social purposes as part of their corporate culture. Indeed,
the GC has done best where companies have created mechanisms of
internal communication that permit employees to comment on and
report how their own work relates to the implementation of the
nine principles – Novartis and Volvo being exemplars. On "internal
branding" of this sort, see Bernard Stamler, "Companies are Developing Brand Messages as a Way to Inspire Loyalty among Employees," *New York Times*, July 5, 2001. In the case of developing
country firms, their rationale for participating also includes a belief
about what is expected of aspiring global corporate players, and in
some cases a perceived opportunity for them to navigate domestically around the dictates of their own governmental bureaucracies.
(Based on interviews with participants.)

62 "Statoil Signs Agreement with ICEM," *Europe Energy*, Mar. 30,
2001.

63 www.melbourne.vic.gov.au/cityplan/infopage.cfm.

64 The distinction between the two approaches is discussed at greater
length in John Gerard Ruggie, "The Theory and Practice of Learning Networks: Corporate Social Responsibility and the Global
Compact," *Journal of Corporate Citizenship*, 5 (Spring 2002).

65 In contrast, the General Assembly has endorsed Annan's approach
to social partnerships, including the Global Compact, in "Towards
Global Partnerships," A/Res/56/76 (Jan. 24, 2002).

66 For a good discussion of the difficulties, see Andrew Clapham, "On
Complicity," in Marc Henzelin and Robert Roth (eds), *Le Droit
pénal à l'épreuve de l'internationalisation* (forthcoming).

67 David E. Rosenbaum, "Senate Deletes Higher Mileage Standard in
Energy Bill," *New York Times*, Mar. 14, 2002. The final vote was
62–38 against.

68 This concept is due to Charles Sabel, Dara O'Rourke and Archon
Fung, "Ratcheting Labor Standards: Regulation for Continuous
Improvement in the Global Workplace," John F. Kennedy School of

Government, Harvard University, KSG Working Paper no. 00–010, May 2, 2000.

69 Andrew C. Revkin, "Forget Nature: Even Eden is Engineered," *New York Times*, Aug. 20, 2002; and Michael E. Conroy, "Can Advocacy-Led Certification Systems Transform Global Corporate Practices? Evidence and Some Theory," University of Massachusetts, Amherst, Political Economy Research Institute, DPE-01-07, Sept. 2001. Conroy claims that the total acreage is more than 5%, and he points out that home improvement centers like Home Depot appear willing to pay a premium for FSC certified lumber. Home Depot got into the act in the first place because activists chose to boycott it to gain leverage over the timber companies, which lack sufficient public personae to be vulnerable to consumer pressure. All major US home improvement outlets participate in the FSC.

70 Conroy, "Can Advocacy-Led Certification Systems Transform Global Corporate Practices?"

71 Andrew King and Michael J. Lenox, "Industry Self-Regulation without Sanctions: The Chemical Industry's Responsible Care Program," *Academy of Management*, 43 (Aug. 2000).

72 Amy Domini, *Socially Responsible Investing: Making a Difference and Making Money* (Chicago: Dearborn Trade, 2001).

73 Commission of the European Communities, "Promoting a European Framework for Corporate Social Responsibility," Brussels: COM [2001] 366 final (July 18, 2001). The OECD itself has issued guidelines for transnational corporations, but there is little evidence that companies have paid much attention to them; *The OECD Guidelines for Multinational Enterprises, Revision 2000* (Paris: OECD, 2000).

74 Barry James, "Action Plan of Summit Looks Weak to Activists," *International Herald Tribune*, Sept. 3, 2002.

75 Some of these partnerships fall into the broader category of "global public policy networks," tri-sectoral efforts that also include the World Commission on Dams, the Climate Action Network and the Roll-Back-Malaria campaign, among others; see Wolfgang H. Reinicke and Francis Deng, *Critical Choices: The United Nations, Networks, and the Future of Global Governance* (Ottawa: International Development Research Center, 2000).

76 The World Economic Forum plans to publish an annual Global Gov-
    ernance Report, which will assess the respective contributions that
    various sectors of society are making to solving global problems;
    www.weforum.org/site/homepublic.nsf/Content/Global+
    Governance+Task+Force.
77 Julia Finch, "Anglo Calls for Help on Aids," *Guardian* (London),
    Aug. 17, 2002.
78 "These companies have concluded that limits on carbon dioxide
    and other greenhouse, or heat-trapping, gases are inevitable. . . .
    And to plan long-term investments, they want the predictability
    that comes from quick adoption of clear rules": Andrew C. Revkin
    and Neela Banerjee, "Energy Executives Urge Voluntary Greenhouse-
    Gas Limits," *New York Times*, Aug. 1, 2001. The companies in-
    cluded the Royal Dutch/Shell Group, BP, several power-generating
    companies – and Enron, which hoped to capture the global permits
    trading business.
79 Marina Ottaway, "Corporatism Goes Global: International Organ-
    izations, Nongovernmental Organizations Networks, and Trans-
    national Business," *Global Governance*, 7 (Sept./Dec. 2001). The
    referent is not corporations, of course, but the system of govern-
    ance that closely integrated elements of the state, business and peak
    labor associations to manage the early twentieth-century breakdown
    of capitalism in several European countries, including Germany and
    Italy.
80 The major work in this genre is David Held, *Democracy and the
    Global Order: From the Modern State to Cosmopolitan Govern-
    ance* (Cambridge: Polity, 1995); and, more recently, David Held,
    "Law of States, Law of Peoples: Three Models of Sovereignty,"
    Legal Theory, 8, no. 1 (2002).

5

Global Governance and Democratic Accountability

Robert O. Keohane

Globalization in the contemporary world means that transnational relationships are both extensive and intensive.[1] States and other organizations exert effects over great distances; people's lives can be fundamentally changed, or ended, as a result of decisions made only days or moments earlier, thousands of miles away. In other words, interdependence is high.

States remain the most powerful actors in world politics, but it is no longer even a reasonable simplification to think of world politics simply as politics among states. A larger variety of other organizations, from multinational corporations to non-governmental organizations, exercise authority and engage in political action across state boundaries. Increasingly extensive networks of communication and affiliation link people in different societies, even when they do not belong to the same formal organization. Some of these networks are benign; others are designed to achieve nefarious purposes such as drug smuggling and money laundering, while members of still others seek to destroy societies or groups of people whom they fear or hate.

Interdependence without any organized government would lead actors to seek to solve their own problems by imposing costs on others. In response, those of their targets who could rationally retaliate – and perhaps some for whom retaliation would be less rational – would do so. The result, familiar in times of war or severe economic strife, would be conflict.

Seeking to ameliorate such conflict, states have for over a century sought to construct international institutions to enable them to cooperate when they have common or complementary interests.[2] That is, they have established rudimentary institutions of governance, bilaterally, regionally, or globally. These attempts at governance, including global governance, are a natural result of increasing interdependence. They also help to create the conditions for further development of the networks of interdependence that are commonly referred to as globalization.[3]

Since states do not monopolize channels of contact among societies, they cannot hope to monopolize institutions of global governance, even those that they have formally established, such as the World Bank, International Monetary Fund and World Trade Organization. States have a privileged position in these organizations, since they founded them, constitute their membership, monopolize voting rights, and provide continuing financial support. Except in the European Union, states also retain the legal authority to implement the decisions of international organizations in domestic law. Yet the entities whose activities are regulated include firms as well as states; and non-governmental organizations play an active role in lobbying governments and international institutions, and in generating publicity for the causes they espouse. NGOs are typically more single-minded and agile than states, which gives them advantages in media struggles. Equally important, religious organizations and movements command the allegiance of billions of people.

The complexity of these patterns of politics makes it very difficult to trace causal relationships and determine patterns of influence. This complexity also makes normative analysis difficult. Emerging patterns of governance are new, and operate at multiple levels. Globalization makes some degree of global-level regulation essential, but both institutions and loyalties are much deeper at local and national levels. Hence it is not clear what principles and practices that are justified domestically would be appropriate at a world scale. Governance can be defined as the making and implementation of rules, and the exercise of power, within a given domain of activity. "Global governance" refers to rule making and power exercise at a global scale, but not necessarily by entities authorized by general agreement to act. Global governance can be exercised by states, religious organizations, and business corporations, as well as by intergovernmental and non-governmental organizations. Since there is no global government, global governance involves strategic interactions among entities that are not arranged in formal hierarchies. Since there is no global constitution, the entities that wield power and make rules are often not authorized to do so by general agreement. Therefore their actions are often not regarded as legitimate by those who are affected by them.

We live in a democratic era, and I share the widespread belief that rules are only legitimate if they conform to broadly democratic principles, appropriately adapted for the context. In democratic theory, individuals are regarded as inherently equal in fundamental rights, and political power is granted to officials by the people, who can withdraw that authority in accordance with constitutional arrangements. The legitimacy of an official action in a democracy depends in part on whether the official is accountable. Hence a key question of global governance involves the types and practices of accountability that are appropriate at this scale. The key question addressed in this article is: what do democratic principles, properly adapted, imply about desirable patterns of accountability in world politics? Which entities should be held accountable, to whom, in what ways? And from a policy standpoint, what do these normative judgments imply about "accountability gaps" – situations in which actual practice differs greatly from a desirable state of affairs?

Part II of this article discusses the concept of accountability, as related to global governance. Part III discusses the various entities that we might want to hold accountable, and how to do this. Contrary to what one might believe on the basis of much writing on the subject, intergovernmental organizations, along with weak states, seem among the most accountable entities in world politics. Corporations, transgovernmental networks, religious organizations and movements, terrorist networks, and powerful states are much less accountable. If we believe in accountability, as I do, we need especially to pay attention to states. How can powerful states be held more accountable in world politics?

Before getting to these arguments, which constitute the heart of this article, it seems important to put the issue of accountability into the context of an interpretation of global society and the global system. It would otherwise be too easy to sketch a highly idealized view of the world. Such a conception is very helpful in thinking about fundamental normative principles, as in the profoundly important work of John Rawls,[4] but it is not adequate if one's purpose is to critique actual situations in world politics. To make such a critique, one needs to sketch out institutional arrangements that satisfy our normative criteria to the extent feasible given the realities of world politics. Although these institutions may be normatively much superior to the actual state of affairs, they may nevertheless fall well short of the arrangements that would fully satisfy abstract normative demands.[5] I therefore begin in part I by contrasting the concept of a "universal global society" with the reality: that world politics as a whole lacks universally accepted values and institutions. In reality, many people and groups in the contemporary world not only hold values that are antithetical to those of others, but seek forcibly to make others' practices conform to their own preferences. Attempts to increase accountability in world politics must take account of the airplane assassins of 9/11, their confederates, and their supporters. Political theory will not be credible if it demands that good people enter into what is in effect a suicide pact.[6]

Robert O. Keohane

I Non-universal global society within a global system

David Held has recently outlined in a very sophisticated way a vision of three models of sovereignty: classic, liberal, cosmopolitan. For Held, there has been movement over the past century from classic to liberal sovereignty. In liberal conceptions of sovereignty, legitimacy is not conferred automatically by control. Indeed, institutions that limit state authority have been developed. Moving beyond liberal sovereignty, Held envisages a prospective movement to cosmopolitan law and governance. Multilevel governance, including governance at the global level, will be "shaped and formed by an overarching cosmopolitan legal framework."[7]

This is an attractive vision, somewhat more ambitious than my own call two years ago to create "working institutions for a [global] polity of unprecedented size and diversity."[8] Both visions, however, would be much more attainable if global society were universal. Twenty-five years ago, Hedley Bull drew an important conceptual distinction between society and system. The states in an international society, for Bull, are "conscious of certain common interests and common values." They "conceive themselves to be bound by a common set of rules in their relations with one another, and share in the working of common institutions."[9] States in an international system that is not an international society do not share common values or work together in international institutions. "When Cortes and Pizarro parleyed with the Aztec and Inca kings [and] when George III sent Lord Macartney to Peking ... this was outside the framework of any shared conception of an international society of which the parties on both sides were members with like rights and duties."[10] However, Bull believed that the European states system had become, by the 1970s, an international society.

Since in the contemporary world entities other than states help to compose society, it seems more appropriate to speak now of global rather than international society. But 9/11 should make us be cautious about believing that global society is becoming universalized. Terrorists have brought sudden external violence and the fear of such violence back into our lives with a vengeance, and the security-seeking, force-wielding state has not been far behind. We therefore need to remind ourselves that a universal global society remains a dream, and one that may be receding from view rather than becoming closer. An increasingly globalized world society has indeed been developing, but it exists within a violence-prone system, both international and transnational. The world is not neatly divided into "zones of peace" and "zones of turmoil,"[11] or areas of "complex interdependence" and "realism."[12] Relationships of peaceful exchange among societies, and violent conflict involving non-state actors, can occur in the same physical spaces.

Human rights advocates have long been aware that a universal global society is more aspiration than reality. The torturers and mass murderers of the world do not share fundamental values with committed and humane democrats. In the wake of 9/11 we have become acutely aware of terrorists' attempts to kill other people, personally unknown to them, who merely stand for hated values or live in states whose policies the terrorists oppose. Perhaps even more soberly, we realize that millions of people cheered or at least sought to justify the evil deeds of 9/11.

On a global scale, common values are lacking. The Taliban did not try to emulate the social organization of Western society, and in fact rejected much of it, such as the practice of enabling women to live public lives. Many fundamentalist religious people do not share – indeed, reject – secular ideals such as those of pluralist democracy. Indeed, one reason that democratic values are not spreading universally is that dogmatic religions claiming exclusive access to comprehensive ultimate truth contain fundamentally anti-democratic elements. Their claim of comprehensiveness means that they assert authority over issues involving the governance of human affairs. Their claim of exclusive access to ultimate truth means that they appeal for authority not to human experience, science or public opinion but to established authority or privileged knowledge of the divine, and they reject accountability to publics and human institutions. Insofar as people believe that power is legitimated by divine authority, they will not be drawn toward liberal democracy.

We must unfortunately conclude that the vision of a universal global society is a mirage. There is indeed a global society: common values and common institutions are not geographically bounded. But the global society in which we live is not universal: it does not include members of al-Qaeda, suicide bombers, or substantial elements of the populations of US allies such as Saudi Arabia and Pakistan. It also excludes other fundamentalists who believe that as the "chosen people" they have special rights and privileges. People with these beliefs may belong to global societies of their own, but they do not belong to the same global society as do those of us who believe in liberal and democratic values. To genuinely belong to an open global society, one must accept others, with very different beliefs about ultimate truth and the good life, as participants, as long as they follow principles of reciprocity in accordance with fair procedural rules.[13]

Even a universal global society would propose a challenge to global governance under the best of circumstances, and it would be difficult to implement a cosmopolitan vision. If globalization of public authority occurred, individual citizens would have few incentives to try to monitor governments' behavior. Indeed, the larger the polity, the more individuals can rationally be ignorant, since each person's actions would have so little effect on policies. That is, the very size of a global polity would create immense incentive problems for voters – in mass election campaigns it would seem pointless to most voters to invest in acquiring information when one's own vote would count, relatively speaking, for so little. It would also be hard, without political parties that operated on a global scale, or a coherent civil society, to aggregate interests and coherently articulate claims. Even a universal global society would lack a strong civil society with robust communication patterns and strong feelings of solidarity with others in the society.

We see these difficulties in the European Union, which is a highly favorable situation, with common democratic values and democratic institutions such as the European Parliament. But the European Union remains largely a set of intergovernmental and supranational institutions supported by a pact among elites, without deep loyalty from the publics of member countries. Even after 45 years of the European Community, it lacks a broad sense of collective identity and mutual support.

Recognizing these realities, sophisticated proponents of greater global governance understand that cosmopolitan democracy cannot be based on a strict analogy with domestic democratic politics, and they do not rely exclusively on electoral accountability. They recognize that even in constitutional democracies, many other kinds of accountability exist, including hierarchical and supervisory accountability, legal accountability (interpreted by courts), and peer accountability among government agencies that compete with one another. Even in the absence of institutionalized accountability mechanisms, reputational accountability can also play a role.[14]

Reliance on diversified types of accountability is supported by the experience of the EU. There is significant accountability in the EU, but electoral accountability, involving the European Parliament, is only part of the picture. EU institutions are accountable to governments; agencies within governments are held accountable to one another through the process of "comitology"; a considerable degree of transparency holds participants, much of the time, accountable to the public through the media. In the EU, political authority and forms of government have become "diffused."[15] As Anne-Marie Slaughter puts it, "disaggregating the State makes it possible to disaggregate sovereignty as well."[16]

In the absence of a universal global society, cosmopolitan democracy is very unlikely on a global scale. Disaggregating the state seems like a recipe for self-destruction when faced with al-Qaeda. Indeed, the strong tendency in the United States since 9/11 has been to consolidate and centralize authority. Transgovernmental

Robert O. Keohane

networks of cooperation against terrorism will play a role, but they will be accompanied by stronger, more aggregated states. Powerful states will seek to link the various levels of governance more coherently rather than to differentiate them or to allow themselves only to serve as elements of a broader structure of cosmopolitan governance. They will tighten control of their borders and surveillance of people within those borders.

The overall result will be a *system* in Bull's sense. Globalization, implying a high level of interdependence, will continue. At a superficial level, most states may remain in a universal international society, accepting common institutions and rules. They can hardly do otherwise if they are to receive political recognition, be allowed freely to trade, and attract investment, much less to be recipients of aid. But acceptance of common global values within societies will be more uneven. No set of common values and institutions will be universally accepted. Global society will therefore be not universal but rather partial. It will exist within the context of a broader international and transnational system, in which both states and non-state actors will play crucial roles.

What will this society-within-system look like? Of course, we don't know – anything said on this subject is speculation. However, five features of this society-within-system can very tentatively be suggested:

1   Large parts of the world will remain in the imagined global society of pre-9/11 times. Indeed, some parts of the world formerly outside this society – such as China and Russia – may well move into it, even at an accelerated rate in response to terrorist threats. Within this sphere, "complex interdependence"[17] and "soft power"[18] will remain important.

2   The fundamental values of substantial populations will be antithetical to one another – especially wherever fundamentalist versions of exclusivist, messianic religions, claiming that their doctrines are comprehensive, prevail in one society. Judaism, Christianity and Islam are all subject to such interpretations.

People who believe that their doctrines alone represent revealed truth have often in history been ill-disposed toward people with different beliefs, and the present seems no exception. Relatively few societies now are dominated by people professing such beliefs, but there is a danger that the number of such societies will increase. Between societies dominated by such people and democratic societies there will not be a common global society – only a system of interactions.[19]

3   Force will continue to be fragmented, controlled mostly by states, but sometimes in the hands of small groups that need not control large amounts of contiguous territory.

4   Within the open global society – the world of complex interdependence – progress toward the cosmopolitan ideal may well occur. Common rules and practices will develop on the basis of procedural agreement, as suggested by the work of Jürgen Habermas or John Rawls.[20]

5   But in the wider system, the cosmopolitan ideal will be unrealistic even as an ideal. Coercion and bargaining will be the chief means of influence, not persuasion and emulation. Hence the state will remain a central actor. Power will not be diffused. Furthermore, territoriality may well be strengthened. For instance, we are now seeing strong pressures to re-establish controls over national borders in the US and in Europe.

II   Governance and the accountability gap

An accountability relationship is one in which an individual, group or other entity makes demands on an agent to report on his or her activities, and has the ability to impose costs on the agent. We can speak of an authorized or institutionalized accountability relationship when the requirement to report, and the right to sanction, are mutually understood and accepted. Other accountability relationships are more contested. In such situations, certain individuals, groups, or entities claim the right to hold agents accountable, but

Robert O. Keohane

the agents do not recognize a corresponding obligation. I refer to the actor holding an agent accountable as a "principal" when the accountability relationship is institutionalized. When the relationship is not institutionalized, I refer to the actor seeking to hold an agent accountable as a "would-be principal." Much of the politics of accountability involves struggles over who should be accepted as a principal.[21]

Democratic accountability within a constitutional system is a relationship in which power wielders are accountable to broad publics. Democratic accountability in world politics could be conceptualized as a hypothetical system in which agents whose actions made a sufficiently great impact on the lives of people in other societies would have to report to those people and be subject to sanctions from them.[22] But accountability need not be democratic. Indeed, it can also be hierarchical (in which subordinates are accountable to superiors) or pluralistic (as in Madisonian constitutionalism, in which different branches of government are accountable to one another). Actual systems of accountability in constitutional democracies combine all three syndromes of accountability: democratic, hierarchic, and pluralistic. As noted above, they rely on a number of different mechanisms, not just on hierarchy and elections. They also rely on horizontal supervision (checks and balances), fiscal and legal controls, peer review, markets, and general concerns about reputation.

Normatively, from the perspective of democratic theory, what justifies demands that an agent be held accountable by some person or group? Three different sets of justifications are commonly enunciated:

(a) *Authorization* Hobbes, and many others, have emphasized that the process by which one entity authorizes another to act may confer rights on the authorizer and obligations on the agent.[23]

(b) *Support* Those who provide financial or political support to a ruler have a claim to hold the ruler accountable. As in the

140

American Revolution, a basic democratic claim is "no taxation without representation."

(c) *Impact* It is often argued, as David Held has said, that "those who are 'choice-determining' for some people [should be] fully accountable for their actions."[24]

Authorization and support are the basis for what I will call internal accountability. They create capabilities to hold entities accountable because the principal is providing legitimacy or financial resources to the agent. This is "internal" accountability since the principal and agent are institutionally linked to one another. Since providing authorization and support creates means of influence, such influence can be used to close any "accountability gap" that may open up between valid normative arguments for internal accountability and actual practice. Nevertheless, much of the literature on accountability, and much anti-globalization talk from Right and Left, focuses exclusively on internal accountability. Globalization, and international institutions, are said to threaten democracy.[25]

In my view, however, the most serious normative problems arise with respect to what I call external accountability: accountability to people outside the acting entity, whose lives are affected by it. African farmers may suffer or prosper as a result of World Bank policies; economic opportunities of people in the India area are affected by the strategies of IBM and Microsoft; Afghans are liberated, displaced, or destroyed by United States military action. The normative question arises in these situations: should the acting entity be accountable to the set of people it affects? This is a very difficult normative question. Merely being affected cannot be sufficient to create a valid claim. If it were, virtually nothing could ever be done, since there would be so many requirements for consultation, and even veto points. I do not seek to resolve this issue here, but I note it as a problem that political philosophers should address. Perhaps the law of torts will be useful here. "In every instance, before negligence can be predicated of a given act, back of the act must be sought and found a duty to the individual complaining."[26] To develop a theory of external accountability, it may be necessary to construct a theory of the duties that parties owe to one another in a poorly institutionalized but increasingly globalized world.

If we determine that a group affected by some set of actions has a valid claim on the acting entity, we can ask the empirical question: in practice, can it effectively demand the accountability that it deserves? If not, there is an accountability gap. In the rest of this article, I am concerned principally with external accountability gaps and how they might be closed.[27]

In general, rulers dislike being held accountable. To be sure, they may often have reasons to submit to accountability mechanisms. In a democratic or pluralistic system, accountability may be essential to maintain the confidence of the public; and in any system, some degree of accountability may be necessary to maintain the credibility of the agent. That is, other dimensions of power may be more important to the ruler than lack of accountability.[28] Furthermore, constitutional systems may be designed to limit abuses of power without reducing the amount of influence the leaders have when action is necessary. But we can expect power-holders to seek to avoid accountability when they can do so without jeopardizing other goals. And in the absence of a constitutional system, *the ability to avoid being held externally accountable can be viewed as one dimension of power*. Discussing accountability without focusing on issues of power would be like discussing motivations of corporate leaders without mentioning money.

III   Accountability in system and society

The mixed society-within-system that I am projecting yields mixed implications for accountability. Internal accountability will be strong, but external accountability will be weak. It almost goes without saying that where conflicts of interest are pronounced, powerful states will not let themselves be held accountable to their adversaries. The United States is not going to be held accountable for its anti-terrorism tactics to al-Qaeda. It is also true that asymmetries of power attenuate accountability. Europe is not going to be held accountable for its immigration policies to the countries of origin of would-be immigrants. Only when they have interests in holding others accountable – as on trade policies in the WTO – are powerful states disposed to let themselves be held accountable.

Yet demands for external accountability will continue to be made against states, intergovernmental organizations, corporations, and other entities viewed as powerful. These demands will largely be made by non-state actors and advocacy networks – hence I speak of "transnational accountability." Meeting these demands, to some extent, will be essential to the legitimacy of institutional arrangements within global society, since many of these claims for accountability will be widely viewed as having some elements of validity.

With respect to transnational accountability, two sets of questions then arise: (1) With respect to which entities are there significant accountability gaps? (2) What types of external accountability could be applicable to these entities?

Transnational accountability: entities

Consider the entities conventionally held accountable on a transnational basis. The most prominent, judging from demonstrations, press coverage, and even scholarly articles, are major intergovernmental organizations concerned with economic globalization: the European Union, World Bank, International Monetary Fund, and the World Trade Organization. These organizations are major targets of demands for accountability. They certainly have deficiencies in accountability. They do not meet democratic standards of accountability as applied in the best-functioning democracies of our era. But ironically, these entities seem to me to be relatively accountable compared to other important global actors.

The European Union is *sui generis*, since it is so much stronger and more elaborately institutionalized than traditional international organizations. Its members have pooled their sovereignty, giving up both a veto over many decisions and the right to decide whether an EU decision will become part of their own domestic law. The EU may or may not evolve into a sovereign state, but in its current condition it lies somewhere between an international organization and a state. As noted above, the EU combines traditional accountability of the bureaucracy to governments with a variety of other forms of accountability, including elections to the European Parliament and multiple forums in which governmental departments can query their counterparts on issues ranging from agriculture to finance.

Traditional international organizations are internally accountable to states on the basis of authorization and support. They have to be created by states and they require continuing financial support from states. Externally, there are significant accountability gaps. Indeed, many poor people affected by the policies of the IMF, World Bank and the WTO have no direct ability to hold these organizations accountable. Nevertheless, there is a vaguely held notion that these people should have some say in what these organizations do – that the "voices of the poor," in the World Bank's phrase, should be heard. That is, many people feel that these organizations should be externally as well as internally accountable.

Various NGOs purporting to speak for affected people, and principles that would help these people, gain legitimacy on the basis of this widespread belief. One result of their endeavors is that the decision-making processes of multilateral organizations have become remarkably more transparent. The World Bank in particular has done a great deal to incorporate NGOs into its decision-making processes.[29] Indeed, in transparency multilateral organizations now compare well to the decision-making processes of most governments, even some democratic governments. When their processes are not transparent, the chief source of non-transparency is governmental pressure for confidentiality. But the decentralization and discord characteristic of world politics mean that these organizations cannot keep secrets very well. Important negotiations, such as those about the Multilateral Agreement on Investment several years ago, are almost bound to "leak." And their leaders spend much of their time trying to answer charges against their organizations, seeking to persuade constituencies that the organizations are actually both constructive and responsive.

Multilateral organizations are therefore anything but "out of control bureaucracies," accountable to nobody.[30] Indeed, the real problem seems to me quite the opposite. These organizations are subject to accountability claims from almost everybody, but in the last analysis they are in fact accountable, through internal processes, only to a few powerful states and the European Union. NGOs and other would-be principals demand accountability. But these NGOs are weak compared to governments, to which the multilateral organizations are chiefly accountable. When these would-be principals lose the battle due to their institutionally weak positions, they condemn the multilateral organizations as "unaccountable." Their real targets are powerful governments of rich countries, perhaps multinational corporations, or even global capitalism – but it is the multilateral organizations that are damaged by the NGO attacks.

What the controversies indicate is not that the intergovernmental organizations are unaccountable, but that accountability is a distributional issue. The issue is not so much: are these organizations accountable? The answer to that question is yes. They are internally accountable to the states that authorized their creation and that provide financial support, and to a lesser extent they are accountable to NGOs and the media. The real issues are whether the balance of internal and external accountability is justifiable, and whether multilateral organizations are accountable to the right groups. NGOs make a normative claim for accountability to groups that are affected, or for accountability to principles such as "sustainable development" or "human rights." In other words, external accountability claims based on the impact of these organizations compete with internal accountability claims, largely by governments, based on authorization and support. These are serious issues, but they are not issues of "lack of accountability" as much as issues of "accountability to whom?" Different types of accountability favor different accountability holders. Once again, accountability is largely a matter of power.

Ironically, intergovernmental organizations have been the principal targets of people demanding external accountability because they are weak and visible. They are good targets because they do not have strong constituencies, and it is much easier to see how they could be reformed than to reform more powerful entities such as multinational corporations or states.

It seems to me that the external accountability gaps are greatest with respect to entities that are not conventionally held accountable on a transnational basis. Six sets of such entities can be mentioned:

1 *Multinational corporations* Multinational corporations are held internally accountable, with more or less success, to their shareholders, who authorize action and provide support. But their actions also have enormous effects on other people. The "anti-globalization movement" is right to be concerned about corporate power, even if its proposed remedies seem incoherent. If we are concerned about the effects of powerful entities on powerless people, we scholars should be asking how to hold corporations accountable – as national governments in capitalist societies have sought to hold corporations accountable for over a century. The effects are particularly pronounced for media conglomerates, but we have not focused on them. Globalization means that it is more difficult for national governments to hold corporations accountable than in the past. Why isn't our field paying more attention?[31]

2 *Transgovernmental and private sector networks*[32] Anne-Marie Slaughter has argued that these networks – such as those

linking securities regulators or central bankers – lead to "disaggregated sovereignty" and that, on the whole, this is a benign development.[33] I am much less sanguine than she is about disaggregated sovereignty being compatible with meaningful accountability. Disaggregating sovereignty makes it much more difficult to identify the locus of decisions. Since these networks are often informal, they are not very transparent. Institutionalized arrangements that would structure internal accountability are lacking, and it is often hard for groups that are affected to identify those effects and demand external accountability.

3   *The Roman Catholic Church* The Vatican has a secretive, authoritarian structure, and is not very accountable to any human institutions or groups. The Church in a democratic society, such as the United States, has to be much more accountable if it is to retain the active allegiance of its members. In the pedophilia scandal in the United States in 2002, accountability was the central issue.

4   *Mass religious movements* without hierarchical organizations. Fundamentalist Islamic movements fall into this category. Unlike the situation of the Roman Catholic Church, there is no hierarchical organization to hold accountable. Who holds imams who preach support for terrorism accountable?

5   *Covert terrorist networks* such as al-Qaeda. These networks are almost by definition not externally accountable. They do not accept the responsibility of identifying themselves, much less responding to questions or accepting others' right to sanction them. They cannot be "held accountable," although they can be punished.

6   *Powerful states* The doctrine of sovereignty has traditionally served to protect states from external accountability, although it has not necessarily protected weak states from accountability to the strong.[34] Multilateral institutions are designed to make states accountable to each other, if not to outsiders. Even moderately powerful states, however, can resist external

accountability on many issues. It has been notably difficult for the United Nations to hold Israel accountable for its military actions on the West Bank. Egypt and Saudi Arabia have not been held accountable to the victims of the terrorists whose supporters they have often encouraged. And most of all, extremely powerful states seem virtually immune from accountability if they refuse to accept it. The United States is of course the chief case in point.[35]

Non-governmental organizations pose a more difficult issue. In an earlier version of this chapter I listed NGOs as a seventh type of entity operating in world politics that should be held more accountable. Indeed, they are often not very transparent. Perhaps more seriously, their legitimacy and their accountability are disconnected. Their claims to a legitimate voice over policy are based on the disadvantaged people for whom they claim to speak, and on the abstract principles that they espouse. But they are internally accountable to wealthy, relatively public-spirited people in the United States and other rich countries, who do not experience the results of their actions. Hence there is a danger that they will engage in symbolic politics, satisfying to their internal constituencies but unresponsive to the real needs of the people whom they claim to serve.

On the other hand, NGOs, on the whole, only wield influence through persuasion and lobbying: they do not directly control resources. Apart from their moral claims and media presence, they are relatively weak. They are highly vulnerable to threats to their reputations. Weakness, as we have seen, ameliorates problems of accountability. My ironic conclusion is that we should not demand strong internal accountability of relatively weak NGOs – the proverbial "two kooks, a letterhead, and a fax machine." But as a particular NGO gains influence, it can exert effects, for good or ill, on people not its members. At this point, it can be as legitimately held externally accountable as other powerful entities that operate in world politics.[36]

The external accountability of states

States are powerful and are often not externally accountable. But institutions of multilateralism exist that hold them accountable on some issues. If we care about accountability, we should inquire as to how such institutions could be extended, and made more effective.

We should begin by recognizing, as Rousseau did, that internal democracy will not assure accountability to outsiders whom the powerful democracy affects.[37] The United States, Israel, and other democracies are internally accountable but on key issues are not externally accountable. David Held has astutely pointed out that the external accountability problem may even be greater as a result of democracy: "arrogance has been reinforced by the claim of the political elites to derive their support from that most virtuous source of power – the demos."[38]

Yet three mechanisms of external accountability apply to states. First, weak countries that depend economically on the decisions of richer countries are subject to demands for fiscal accountability. Albert Hirschman pointed out over 50 years ago that foreign trade, when it produces benefits, generates an "influence effect."[39] As I have repeatedly emphasized, accountability is a power-laden concept. Power comes from asymmetrical interdependence in favor of the power wielder.[40]

The implication of the influence effect is that if rich countries are genuinely interested in holding poor countries accountable, they will give more aid. Dramatically increased efforts to increase the benefits that poor countries receive from globalization would create an influence effect, making it easier to hold these countries accountable for their actions. Of course, for the poor countries such generosity would be problematic, precisely because it would make them more dependent on the rich.

A second mechanism of external accountability relies on the pockets of institutionalized accountability that currently exist in world politics. States that are members of regional organizations such as the European Union are subject to demands for accountability from their peers. And states that have joined organizations such as the WTO or the new International Criminal Court are subject to legal accountability with respect to specified activities. Europe, the United States, Japan and other rich countries are targets of demands for accountability in trade, with their agricultural subsidies and protection of old industries such as steel serving as prominent examples. The extension of some degree of accountability to powerful states, through multilateral institutions, offers a glimmer of hope. But we should remember that these powerful states do not accept accountability for its own sake, but chiefly because they gain benefits themselves from these institutions. And as recent US policies on steel and agriculture remind us, powerful democratic states are subject to much more internal than external accountability.

Finally, the most general form of accountability in world politics is reputational. States and other organizations with strong sources of internal loyalty probably rely on external reputation less than organizations, such as most NGOs, that lack broad bases of loyal members. Nevertheless, reputation is the only form of external accountability that appears to constrain the United States with respect to its political-military activities. Reputation is double-edged, since states may seek reputations for being tough bullies as well as for being reliable partners. And the lack of institutionalization of reputational concerns makes reputation a relatively unreliable source of constraint. Yet reputational accountability has some potential significance because reputations of states matter for their other activities. To be effective, states have to be included in the relevant networks.[41] Hence, reputational accountability, weak though it is, is significant.

On any given issue, the United States can typically act unilaterally, dismissing demands for external accountability. Indeed, one of my themes is the weakness of external as opposed to internal accountability, as far as powerful states are concerned. However, the US has many objectives in the world, some of which require voluntary cooperation from others. It would be impossible for the

United States to coerce other states on all issues of concern for it. Failing to cooperate with others leads them to retaliate in one form or another, following practices of reciprocity. More diffusely, damage to the reputation of the United States as a potential cooperator reduces the incentives for others to cooperate with the United States in anticipation of cooperation on some other issues in the future. Most generally, any country playing a long-term leadership role in global governance has a long-term interest in the legitimacy of global governance, as well as in its status as leader. To any sensible US Administration, such concern for leadership would be a constraint – and a reason to let itself be held accountable, to some extent, on other issues.[42]

I have pointed to three sources of external accountability – the need of poor countries for aid, institutionalization in international organizations, and reputational concerns arising from multiple issues for powerful states such as the United States. None is very strong. But we should note that all three sources of accountability are augmented by the political institutions that are part of globalization. Globalization is not a single phenomenon. Some aspects of globalization reflect economic and technological facts that cannot be affected by political action. Action at a distance, and harm at a distance, are more feasible, and frequent, now than ever before. Other aspects of globalization, such as the construction of multilateral institutions and policy networks, and efforts to create public spaces in which persuasion based on reason can occur, require political action: Max Weber's "strong and slow boring of hard boards."[43] It would be tragic if the "anti-globalization" movement succeeded in demolishing or diminishing the institutions and networks developed to cope with globalization, without putting comparable institutions in their place. Since technologically driven globalization will not disappear, such dismantling would reduce accountability and create more opportunities for the irresponsible use of power. Globalization may weaken internal accountability within democracies, but its political institutionalization is a condition for external accountability.

Here is another irony. Opponents of globalization often raise the issue of accountability as an argument against globalization. But they are thinking of a largely imaginary bygone world in which states really controlled their borders and in which democratic governments regulated domestic activities through democratic means. Their imaginary world is the United States during the New Deal, as they would have liked it to evolve – without Nazism, fascism, Communism and World War II. In fact, the choice is not globalization or not, but relatively legitimate globalization with a measure of democratic and pluralistic external accountability over powerful entities, versus illegitimate globalization without such accountability.

Having said all of this, it would nevertheless be naive to believe that the United States will be easy to hold externally accountable. Indeed, for the United States to be held accountable, internal accountability will have to supplement external accountability rather than substituting for it. Those of its own people who are sensitive to world politics will have to demand it, both on the grounds of self-interest and with respect to American values.

In view of contemporary American public attitudes, this hortatory comment does not necessarily offer much hope, at least in the short run. Indeed, my ironic conclusion is that with respect to accountability, the two sworn enemies – al-Qaeda and the United States – have in common their relative lack of accountability, compared to other actors in world politics.

Conclusions

Those of us who would like to see greater democratic and pluralistic accountability in world politics must recognize that global society, while real, will not become universal in the foreseeable future. Too many people believe in the superiority of their own worldviews and deny the obligation to tolerate the views of others. The resulting threats, along with traditional security concerns, help to ensure that powerful states seeking to control territory will continue to assert themselves. Cosmopolitan democracy is a distant ideal, not a feasible option for our time.

We should demand more external accountability of powerful entities engaged in various forms of global governance. Intergovernmental organizations and weak, dependent states are most easily held accountable. We cannot expect to hold shadowy terrorist movements accountable. But we should pay more attention to the accountability of corporations, transgovernmental networks, religious organizations and movements, and powerful states.

The United States especially needs to be held accountable, because its internal democracy cannot be counted on to defend the interests of weak peoples whom American action may harm. Yet it is very difficult to hold the United States accountable, since one dimension of power is that it protects the power-holder from accountability. 9/11 implies more concentration of power and more state action. As a result, the world is further from the ideal of transnational accountability now than most of us recognized before 9/11.

If we recognize that powerful states pose the most serious threats to accountability in world politics, we will see that well-meaning efforts to demand "more accountability" from international organizations can be problematic. As I have argued, "more accountable" often means "accountable to NGOs and advocacy networks," rather than just to governments. Certainly some real benefits could result from making the WTO and the IMF more accountable to a wider range of interests and values. But we should be alert to the prospect that the political result of such a shift would be a reduction of states' interests in such organizations. If states get less benefit from international institutions, they will be less willing to provide resources and to accept demands on them, through these institutions, for accountability. The ultimate result of such well-meaning moves, therefore, could be a weakening of the accountability, limited as it is, that multilateralism imposes on powerful states.

Robert O. Keohane

In the long run global governance will only be legitimate if there is a substantial measure of external accountability. Global governance can impose limits on powerful states and other powerful organizations, but it also helps the powerful, because they shape the terms of governance. In their own long-run self-interest, therefore, powerful states such as the United States should accept a measure of accountability – despite their inclinations to the contrary. As in 1776, Americans should display "a decent respect for the opinions of mankind."

How, then, can we hope to hold powerful entities accountable in world politics? The first point is that to hold powerful states accountable, the world needs more multilateral governance, not less. Indeed, one of my concerns about claims that multilateral organizations are "not accountable" is that weakening these organizations will give powerful governments more ability simply to act as they please. Holding states accountable depends on certain aspects of globalization: those that derive from the existence of significant political institutions with global scope. If leaders of the anti-globalization movement believe that they are fostering equality and progressive policies in world politics by attacking multilateral institutions, they are sadly mistaken.

More fundamentally, holding powerful organizations accountable will require meshing together more effectively mechanisms of internal and external accountability. Global institutions are not strong enough to impose a fully satisfactory measure of external accountability on powerful states, corporations, or religious organizations. Multilateralism is not sufficient to control, in Benjamin Barber's phrase, either Jihad or McWorld.[44] For such control to be exercised, states themselves will have to take action, but in concert with one another.

Only democratic states can be counted on, more or less, to exercise such control on behalf of broad publics. But as we have seen, if those publics are encapsulated within state boundaries, leaders of states will tend to ignore the costs that their policies impose on outsiders. External accountability will be minimal. In

154

the long term, the only remedy for this situation is that networks of connection, and empathy, develop on a global basis so that democratic publics in powerful states demand that the interests of people in weaker states be taken into account. That is, people need to adopt a moral concept of reciprocity as described above, and as articulated by Rawls. To do so they need to renounce doctrines, religious or otherwise, that deny the moral equality of other people, who hold different beliefs. In light of 9/11 it seems utopian to expect people everywhere to accept this moral concept of reciprocity. Yet such a conception is widely shared with successful national states, even within large ones. There is no doubt that the people of the United States as a whole empathized with the people of Oklahoma City in 1995 and of New York City in 2001. At a global level the bonds of connection are much too weak now, even where common societies are well established, to support the level of empathy that we observe within nation-states. But our best hope for cosmopolitan governance in the long run is the construction and strengthening of these personal and social ties.

Our principal task as scholars and citizens who believe in more accountability is to build support within our powerful, rich countries for acceptance of more effective and legitimate multilateral governance to achieve human purposes, for stronger transnational bonds of empathy, and for the increased external accountability that is likely to follow.

Notes

I am grateful to Ruth Grant, David Held, Nannerl O. Keohane, Joseph S. Nye, and Kathryn Sikkink for comments on an earlier version of this chapter, which was originally given as a Miliband Lecture at the London School of Economics, May 17, 2002. Joseph Nye's insights into issues of accountability, which we have discussed in the context of some of our joint writings, have been very important in helping to shape my ideas on this subject. A conference organized by Michael Barnett and Raymond Duvall at the University of Wisconsin in April 2002 helped, through its emphasis on the role of power in global governance, to sharpen my appreciation of the links between accountability and power.

1   David Held, Anthony McGrew, David Goldblatt, and Jonathan Perraton, *Global Transformations: Politics, Economics and Culture* (Cambridge: Polity, 1999).
2   Robert O. Keohane, *After Hegemony: Cooperation and Discord in the World Political Economy* (Princeton: Princeton University Press, 1984).
3   Robert O. Keohane and Joseph S. Nye Jr, *Power and Interdependence*, 3rd edn (New York: Addison-Wesley Longman, 2001), ch. 10.
4   John Rawls, *A Theory of Justice* (Cambridge, Mass.: Belknap Press of Harvard University Press, 1971) and *Political Liberalism* (New York: Columbia University Press, 1993).
5   In *The Law of Peoples* Rawls has sought to move in the direction of sketching what he calls a "realistic utopia." He has, of course, not escaped criticism for allegedly relaxing his principles too much, in order to develop an international law that could be accepted by "decent hierarchical peoples" as well as by liberal democracies. Yet the level of specificity of *The Law of Peoples* is not sufficient to make judgments about which entities in world politics are subject to appropriate procedures for accountability. See John Rawls, *The Law of Peoples* (Cambridge, Mass.: Harvard University Press, 1999).
6   Justice Robert H. Jackson is quoted as having said that the Bill of Rights should not be made into a suicide pact. See, for instance, Richard A. Posner, "Civil Liberties and the Law," *The Atlantic*, Dec. 2001.
7   David Held, "Law of States, Law of Peoples: Three Models of Sovereignty," *Legal Theory*, 8 (2002), p. 33.
8   Robert O. Keohane, "Governance in a Partially Globalized World," *American Political Science Review*, 95 (2001), p. 12.
9   Hedley Bull, *The Anarchical Society: A Study of Order in World Politics* (New York: Columbia University Press, 1977), p. 13.
10 Ibid., p. 15.
11 Max Singer and Aaron Wildavsky, *The Real World Order: Zones of Peace, Zones of Turmoil* (Chatham, N.J.: Chatham House Publishers, 1993).
12 Keohane and Nye, *Power and Interdependence*.

13 Rawls, *Political Liberalism.*

14 For a detailed discussion of types of accountability, see Robert O. Keohane and Joseph S. Nye Jr, "Redefining Accountability for Global Governance," in Miles Kahler and David A. Lake (eds), *Globalizing Authority* (Princeton: Princeton University Press, 2003).

15 David Held, "Law of States, Law of Peoples," p. 38.

16 Anne-Marie Slaughter, "Governing the Economy through Government Networks," in Michael Byers (ed.), *The Role of Law in International Politics* (Oxford: Oxford University Press, 2000), p. 203.

17 Keohane and Nye, *Power and Interdependence.*

18 Joseph S. Nye Jr, *The Paradox of American Power* (New York: Oxford University Press, 2002).

19 In my view, Samuel Huntington overgeneralized his insights about a "clash of civilizations," but he was right to call attention to the importance of the different values to which people from different cultures are committed. Samuel P. Huntington, *The Clash of Civilizations and the Remaking of World Order* (New York: Simon and Schuster, 1996).

20 Jürgen Habermas, *Between Facts and Norms: Contributions to a Discourse Theory of Law and Democracy* (Cambridge, Mass.: MIT Press, 1996); Rawls, *The Law of Peoples.*

21 Robert D. Behn, *Rethinking Democratic Accountability* (Washington DC: Brookings Institution, 2001).

22 Held, "Law of States, Law of Peoples," p. 27.

23 Hannah Pitkin, *The Concept of Representation* (Berkeley: University of California Press, 1972).

24 Held, "Law of States, Law of Peoples," p. 26.

25 Robert A. Dahl, "Can International Organizations be Democratic? A Skeptic's View," in Ian Shapiro and Casiano Hacker-Cordon (eds), *Democracy's Edges* (Cambridge: Cambridge University Press, 1999).

26 Chief Justice McSherry in *W. Va. Central R. Co. v State*, 96 Md. 652, 666; quoted in Chief Justice Benjamin Cardozo's majority opinion in *Palsgraf v Long Island Railroad Company*, 248 N. Y. 339, 162 N.E. 99 (1928).

27 My normative perspective is founded on the impartialist views that stem from Kant, as enunciated recently by such thinkers as Rawls and Habermas. See Rawls, *A Theory of Justice*, and Habermas, *Between Facts and Norms.* It is also cosmopolitan, broadly consistent

with arguments made by David Held, "Globalization, Corporate Practice and Cosmopolitan Social Standards," *Contemporary Political Theory*, 1 (2002), pp. 58–78.

28 Hannah Arendt defined power as "the human ability to act in concert"; Hannah Arendt, *Crises of the Republic* (New York: Harcourt Brace Jovanovich, 1969), p. 143. In democratic, pluralistic societies, the ability to act in concert may require accountability of rulers.
29 I am grateful to Kathryn Sikkink for this point.
30 The reference is to Arendt, *Crises of the Republic*, p. 137, who described bureaucracy as "rule by Nobody."
31 I am not including labor unions, since I do not regard them as powerful transnational actors. They are heavily rooted in domestic society and despite their activity at Seattle and elsewhere in protesting globalization, they have difficulty coordinating their actions on a transnational basis.
32 Robert O. Keohane and Joseph Nye Jr, "Transgovernmental Relations and World Politics," *World Politics*, 27 (1974), pp. 39–62.
33 Slaughter, "Governing the Economy through Government Networks."
34 Stephen D. Krasner, *Sovereignty: Organized Hypocrisy* (Princeton: Princeton University Press, 1999).
35 This is not to say that the United States is immune from influence by other states. It moderated its stance on the Geneva Conventions for prisoners from Afghanistan, and it followed established treaty practice in notifying foreign governments of the incarceration of their nationals in the wake of 9/11. But the ability of outsiders to hold the United States accountable in a meaningful sense is small.
36 For a thoughtful set of discussions of the accountability of NGOs, see *Chicago Journal of International Law* (2002).
37 Stanley Hoffmann, *Janus and Minerva: Essays in the Theory and Practice of International Politics* (Boulder, Colo.: Westview, 1987), p. 43.
38 Held, "Law of States, Law of Peoples," p. 21.
39 Albert Hirschman, *National Power and the Structure of Foreign Trade* (Berkeley: University of California Press, 1945).
40 Keohane and Nye, *Power and Interdependence*.
41 Abram Chayes and Antonia Handler Chayes, *The New Sovereignty: Compliance with International Regulatory Agreements* (Cambridge, Mass.: Harvard University Press, 1995).

42 For a fine discussion of these and related issues, see Nye, *The Paradox of American Power*.

43 Max Weber, *Politics as a Vocation* (1919; Philadelphia: Fortress Press, 1965), p. 55.

44 Benjamin Barber, *Jihad vs. McWorld* (New York: Times Books, 1995).

6

From Executive to
Cosmopolitan Multilateralism

David Held

It is easy to overstate the moment – to overgeneralize from the experience of one event and one time. Thus, for example, we could interpret 9/11 as a, if not the, turning point in the contemporary period; the moment when the project of globalization met the project of mass terrorism, tinged with global radical Islam. Mass terrorism could be thought of as the challenge to globalization and the spread of such values as the rule of law, democracy, and equal liberty. It is a challenge to all these things, of course. But there are other challenges as well, which could be interpreted as broader and deeper. In what follows, I will map some of these.

There is nothing new about globalization. There have been many phases of globalization over the last two millennia including the development of world religions; the Age of Discovery; and the spread of empires. But having recognized this, it is important to note that there is something new about globalization in the current period; that is, about the confluence of change across human activities – economic, political, legal, communicative and environmental. We can trace this by measuring the extent, intensity, velocity and impact of human networks and relations in each of the core domains of activity, and this I have tried to do with Anthony McGrew in *Global Transformations* and other works.[1]

Contemporary globalization shares elements in common with past phases, but is distinguished by unique organizational features, creating a world in which the extensive reach of human relations and networks is matched by its relative high intensity, high velocity and high impact propensity across many facets of social life. The result is the emergence of a global economy, 24-hour trading in financial markets, multinational corporations which dwarf many a country's economic resources, new forms of international law, the development of regional and global governance structures and the creation of global systemic problems – global warming, AIDS, mass terrorism, market volatility, money laundering, the international drugs trade, among other phenomena. A number of striking challenges are posed by these developments.

The challenges of globalization

(1) Contemporary processes of globalization and regionalization create overlapping networks of power which cut across territorial boundaries; as such they put pressure on, and strain, a world order designed in accordance with the Westphalian principle of exclusive sovereign rule over a bounded territory.

(2) The locus of effective political power can no longer be assumed to be simply national governments – effective power is shared and bartered by diverse forces and agencies, public and private, at national, regional and international levels. Moreover, the idea of a self-determining people – or of a political community of fate – can no longer be located within the boundaries of a single nation-state alone. Some of the most fundamental forces and processes which determine the nature of life chances are now beyond the reach of individual nation-states.

A distinctive aspect of this is the emergence of 'global politics' – the increasingly extensive form of political activity. Political decisions and actions in one part of the world can rapidly acquire worldwide ramifications. Sites of political action and/or decision-making can become linked through rapid communications into complex networks of political interaction. Associated with this 'stretching' of politics is a frequent intensification of global processes such that 'action at a distance' permeates the social conditions and cognitive worlds of specific places or policy communities.[2] As a consequence, developments at the global level – whether economic, social or environmental – can acquire almost instantaneous local consequences and vice versa.

The idea of global politics challenges the traditional distinctions between the domestic and the international, and between the territorial and the non-territorial, as embedded in modern conceptions of 'the political'.[3] It highlights the richness and complexity of the interconnections which transcend states and societies in the global order. Global politics today, moreover, is anchored not just in traditional geopolitical concerns but also in a large diversity of economic, social and ecological questions. Pollution, drugs, human rights and terrorism are among an increasing number of transnational policy issues which cut across territorial jurisdictions and existing political alignments, and which require international cooperation for their effective resolution.

Nations, peoples and organizations are linked, in addition, by many new forms of communication which range across borders. The revolution in microelectronics, in information technology and in computers has established virtually instantaneous worldwide links which, when combined with the technologies of the telephone, television, cable and satellite, have dramatically altered the nature of political communication. The intimate connection between 'physical setting', 'social situation' and politics which distinguished most political associations from premodern to modern times has been ruptured; the new communication systems create new experiences, new modes of understanding and new frames of political reference independently of direct contact with particular peoples, issues or events. The speed with which the events of 11 September 2001 ramified across the world and made mass terrorism a global issue is one poignant example.

In the past, nation-states principally resolved their differences over boundary matters by pursuing 'reasons of state' backed by diplomatic initiatives and, ultimately, by coercive means. But this power logic is singularly inadequate to resolve the many complex issues, from economic regulation to resource depletion and environmental degradation, which engender – at seemingly ever greater speeds – an intermeshing of 'national fortunes'. We are, as Kant most eloquently put it, 'unavoidably side by side'. In a world where powerful states make decisions not just for their peoples but for others as well, and where transnational actors and forces cut across the boundaries of national communities in diverse ways, the questions of who should be accountable to whom, and on what basis, do not easily resolve themselves.

(3)   Existing political institutions, national and international, are weakened by three crucial regulatory and political gaps:[4]

- a *jurisdictional* gap – the discrepancy between a regionalized and globalized world and national, separate units of policy-making, giving rise to the problem of externalities such as the degradation of the global commons and who is responsible for them;
- a *participation* gap – the failure of the existing international system to give adequate voice to many leading global actors, state and non-state; and
- an *incentive* gap – the challenges posed by the fact that, in the absence of any supranational entity to regulate the supply and use of global public goods, many states will seek to free ride and/or fail to find durable collective solutions to pressing transnational problems.

(4)   These political disjunctures are conjoined by an additional gap – what might be called a 'moral gap'; that is, a gap defined by:

(a)   a world in which over 1.2 billion people live on less than a dollar a day; 46 per cent of the world's population live on

David Held

less than $2 a day; and 20 per cent of the world's population enjoy 80 per cent of its income (see Wade in this volume); and

(b) commitments and values of, at best, 'passive indifference' to this, marked by UN expenditure per annum of $1.25 billion (plus peacekeeping); US per annum confectionery expenditure of $27 billion; US per annum alcohol expenditure of $70 billion, and US per annum expenditure on cars that is through the roof (over $550 billion).

This is not an anti-America statement, of course. Equivalent European Union figures could have been highlighted.

Seemingly obvious questions arise. Would anyone freely choose such a state of affairs? Would anyone freely choose a distributional pattern of scarce goods and services, leading to hundreds of millions of people suffering serious harm and disadvantage independent of their will and consent (and 50,000 dying every day of malnutrition and poverty-related causes), if the choosers did not already know that they had a privileged stake in the current social hierarchy? Would anyone freely endorse a situation in which the annual cost of supplying basic education to all children is $6 billion, of water and sanitation $9 billion, and of basic health to all $13 billion, while annually $4 billion is spent in the US on cosmetics, nearly $20 billion on jewellery and $17 billion (in the US and Europe) on pet food?[5] Before an impartial court of moral reason (testing the reasonable rejectability of claims), it is hard to see how an affirmative answer to these questions could be defended. That global inequalities spark conflict and contestation can hardly be a surprise, especially given the visibility of the world's lifestyles in an age of mass media.

(5) There has been a shift from relatively discrete national communication and economic systems to their more complex and diverse enmeshment at regional and global levels, and from government to multilevel governance. This can be illustrated by a

number of developments including, most obviously, the rapid emergence of multilateral agencies and organizations. New forms of multilateral politics have been established involving governments, intergovernmental organizations (IGOs) and a wide variety of transnational pressure groups and international non-governmental organizations (INGOs).[6] In addition, there has been a very substantial development in the number of international treaties in force, as well as in the number of international regimes, altering the situational context of states.[7]

To this pattern of extensive political interconnectedness can be added the dense web of activity of the key international policy-making fora, including the summits of the UN, G7 group of industrialized countries, IMF, WTO, EU, APEC (Asia-Pacific Economic Cooperation), ARF (the regional forum of the Association of South East Asian Nations) and MERCOSUR (the Southern Cone Common Market – in Latin America) and many other official and unofficial meetings. In the middle of the nineteenth century there were two or three interstate conferences or congresses per annum; today they number several thousand annually. National government is increasingly locked into an array of global, regional and multilayered systems of governance – and can barely monitor it all, let alone stay in command. Foreign and domestic policy areas have become chronically intermeshed, making the national coordination and control of government policy increasingly problematic.

Interlaced with these political and legal transformations are changes in the world military order. Few states, except perhaps for the US and China, can now contemplate solely unilateralism or neutrality as a credible defence strategy. Global and regional security institutions have become more prevalent as a collectivization of national security has evolved.[8] But it is not just the institutions of defence which have become multinational. The way military hardware is manufactured has also changed. The age of 'national champions' has been superseded by a sharp increase in licensing, co-production agreements, joint ventures, corporate alliances and subcontracting.[9] This means that few countries – not even the United States – can claim to have a wholly autonomous military production capacity. Such a point can be highlighted in connection with key civil technologies, such as electronics, which are vital to advanced weapons systems, and which are themselves the products of highly globalized industries.

Political communities can no longer be conceived, if they ever could with any degree of accuracy, as simply discrete worlds or as self-enclosed political spaces; they are enmeshed in complex structures of overlapping forces, relations and networks. Yet there are few grounds for thinking that a parallel 'globalization' of political identities has taken place. One exception to this is to be found among the elites of the global order – the networks of experts and specialists, senior administrative personnel and transnational business executives – and those who track and contest their activities, the loose constellation of social movements (including the anti-globalization movement), trade unionists and (a few) politicians and intellectuals. But these groups are not typical. Thus we live with a challenging paradox – that governance is becoming increasingly a multilevel, intricately institutionalized and spatially dispersed activity, while representation, loyalty and identity remain stubbornly rooted in traditional ethnic, regional and national communities.[10]

One important qualification needs to be added to the above arguments, one which focuses on generational change. While those who have some commitment to the global order as a whole and to the institutions of global governance constitute a distinct minority, a generational divide is evident. Compared to the generations brought up in the years prior to 1939, those born after World War II are more likely to see themselves as cosmopolitans, to support the UN system and to be in favour of the free movement of migrants and trade. Examining Eurobarometer data and findings from the World Values Survey (involving over seventy countries), Norris concludes that 'cohort analysis suggests that in the long term public opinion is moving in a more international direction.'[11]

Generations brought up with Yahoo!, MTV and CNN affirm this trend and are more likely to have some sense of global identification, although it remains to be seen whether this tendency crystallizes into a majority position and whether it generates a clearly focused political orientation, north, south, east and west.

Hence, the shift from government to multilayered governance, from national economies to economic globalization, is a potentially unstable shift, capable of reversal in some respects and certainly capable of engendering a fierce reaction – a reaction drawing on nostalgia, romanticized conceptions of political community, hostility to outsiders (refugees) and a search for a pure national state (for example, in the politics of Haider in Austria, Le Pen in France and so on). But this reaction itself is likely to be highly unstable, and perhaps a relatively short- or medium-term phenomenon. To understand why this is so, nationalism has to be disaggregated.

(6)   As 'cultural nationalism' nationalism is, and in all likelihood will remain, central to people's identity; however, as political nationalism – the assertion of the exclusive political priority of national identity and the national interest – it cannot deliver many sought-after public goods without seeking accommodation with others, in and through regional and global collaboration. In this respect, only an international or, better still, cosmopolitan outlook can, ultimately, accommodate itself to the political challenges of a more global era, marked by overlapping communities of fate and multilevel/multilayered politics. Unlike political nationalism, cosmopolitanism registers and reflects the multiplicity of issues, questions, processes and problems which affect and bind people together, irrespective of where they were born or reside.

What is cosmopolitanism?

Cosmopolitanism is concerned to disclose the cultural, legal and ethical basis of political order in a world where political communities and states matter, but not only and exclusively. It dates at least to the Stoics' description of themselves as cosmo-politans – 'human beings living in a world of human beings and only incidentally members of polities'.[12] The Stoic emphasis on the morally contingent nature of membership of a political com-munity seems anachronistic after over three hundred years of state development. But what is neither anachronistic nor misplaced is the recognition of the partiality, one-sidedness and limitedness of 'reasons of state' or 'reasons of political community' when judged from the perspective of a world of 'overlapping communities of fate' – where the trajectories of each and every country are tightly entwined. States can be conceived as vehicles to aid the deliv-ery of effective public regulation, equal liberty and social justice, but they should not be thought of as ontologically privileged. Cosmopolitanism today must take this as a starting point, and build a robust conception of the proper basis of political commu-nity and the relations among communities. The Kantian under-standing of this, based on a model of human interaction anchored in co-presence, cannot be an adequate basis for this.[13] Cosmopolitanism needs to be reworked for another age.

What would such a cosmopolitanism amount to? In the space available, it is not possible to unpack adequately what I take to be the multidimensional nature of cosmopolitanism.[14] But it is import-ant to clarify that cosmopolitanism is not at loggerheads with all aspects of state tradition; nor does it deny cultural difference or the enduring significance of national culture. It is not against cultural diversity. Few, if any, contemporary cosmopolitans hold such views.[15] Rather, cosmopolitanism should be understood as the capacity to mediate between national cultures, communities of fate and alternative styles of life. It aims to disclose the basis for dialogue with the traditions and discourses of others with the aim of expanding the horizons of one's own framework of meaning and prejudice.[16] Political agents who can 'reason from the point of view of others' are better equipped to resolve, and resolve fairly, the

challenging transboundary issues that create overlapping communities of fate. The development of this kind of cosmopolitanism
depends on the recognition of three fundamental principles.[17]

The first is that the ultimate units of moral concern are individual human beings, not states or other particular forms of human
association. Humankind belongs to a single moral realm in which
each person is equally worthy of respect and consideration.[18] This
notion can be referred to as the principle of individualist moral
egalitarianism or, simply, egalitarian individualism. To think of
people as having equal moral value is to make a general claim
about the basic units of the world comprising persons as free and
equal beings.[19] This broad position runs counter to the view of
moral particularists that belonging to a given community limits
and determines the moral worth of individuals and the nature of
their autonomy.

The second principle emphasizes that the status of equal worth
should be acknowledged by everyone. It is an attribute of every
living person, and the basis on which each person ought to constitute their relations with others.[20] Each person has an equal stake
in this universal ethical realm and is, accordingly, required to
respect everyone else's status as a basic unit of moral interest.[21]
This second element of contemporary cosmopolitanism can be
called the principle of reciprocal recognition.

The third principle stresses that equality of status and reciprocal
recognition requires that each person should enjoy the impartial
treatment of their claims – that is, treatment based on principles
upon which all could act. Accordingly, cosmopolitanism is a moral
frame of reference for specifying rules and principles that can
be universally shared; and, concomitantly, it rejects as unjust all
those practices, rules and institutions anchored in principles not all
could adopt.[22] At issue is the establishment of impartial principles
and rules that nobody, motivated to establish an uncoerced and
informed agreement, could reasonably reject.[23] The concern is not
overambitious. As one commentator aptly explained:

All the impartiality thesis says is that, if and when one raises questions regarding fundamental moral standards, the court of appeal that one addresses is a court in which no particular individual, group, or country has special standing. Before the court, declaring 'I like it', 'it serves my country', and the like, is not decisive; principles must be defensible to anyone looking at the matter apart from his or her special attachments, from a larger, human perspective.[24]

This larger, open-ended, moral perspective is a device for focusing our thoughts, and a basis for testing the intersubjective validity of our conceptions of the good. It offers a way of exploring principles, norms and rules that might reasonably command agreement.[25]

One such principle is the principle of the avoidance of serious harm and the amelioration of urgent need. This is a principle for allocating priority to the most vital cases of need and, where possible, trumping other, less urgent public priorities until such a time as all human beings enjoy the status of equal moral value, reciprocal recognition, and have the means to participate in their respective political communities and in the overlapping communities of fate which shape their needs and welfare. A social provision which falls short of this can be referred to as a situation of manifest 'harm' in that the recognition of, and potential for, active agency will not have been achieved for all individuals or groups; that is to say, some people would not have adequate access to the effectively resourced capacities which they might make use of in particular circumstances.[26]

I take cosmopolitanism ultimately to connote the ethical and political space which sets out the terms of reference for the recognition of people's equal moral worth, their active agency and what is essential for their autonomy and development – free of urgent need.[27] It builds on principles that all could reasonably assent to in defending ideas which emphasize equal dignity, equal respect, the priority of vital need, and so on. On the other hand, this cosmopolitan point of view must also recognize that the meaning of these cannot be specified once and for all. That is to say, the connotation of these basic ideas cannot be separated from the hermeneutic complexity of traditions, with their temporal and cultural structures. In other words, the meaning of cosmopolitan regulative principles cannot be elucidated independently of an ongoing discussion in public life.[28]

Cosmopolitan institution-building

The principles of egalitarian individualism, reciprocal recognition and impartialist reasoning find direct expression in significant legal and institutional initiatives after World War II and in some of the new forms of regional and global governance. To begin with, the 1948 UN Declaration of Human Rights and subsequent 1966 Covenants of rights raised the principle of egalitarian individualism to a universal reference point: the requirement that each person be treated with equal concern and respect, irrespective of the state in which they were born or brought up, is the central plank of the human rights worldview.[29] In addition, the formal recognition in the UN Declaration of all people as persons with 'equal and inalienable rights', and that this is 'the foundation of freedom, justice and peace in the world', marked a turning point in the development of cosmopolitan legal thinking (UN Declaration, preamble). Single persons are recognized as subjects of international law and, in principle, the ultimate source of political authority.[30]

The tentative acceptance of the equal worth of all human beings finds reinforcement in the acknowledgement of the necessity of a minimum of civilized conduct and of specific limits to violence found in the laws of war and weapons diffusion; in the commitment to the principles of the Nuremberg and Tokyo war crimes tribunals (1945–6, 1946–8), the Torture Convention (1984) and the statute of the International Criminal Court (1998) which outlaws genocide, war crimes and crimes against humanity; in the growing recognition of democracy as the fundamental standard of political legitimacy which finds entrenchment in the International

171

David Held

Bill of Human Rights and regional treaties; in the development of new codes of conduct for IGOs and INGOs, concerning the transparency and accountability of their activities; and in the unprecedented flurry of regional and global initiatives, regimes, institutions, networks and treaties seeking to tackle global warming, ozone depletion, the pollution of oceans and rivers, and nuclear risks, among many other factors.[31]

Yet, while there may be cosmopolitan elements to existing international law and regulation, these have, of course, by no means generated a new deep-rooted structure of cosmopolitan accountability and regulation. The principle of egalitarian individualism may be widely recognized, but it scarcely structures much social and economic policy, north, south, east or west. The principle of universal recognition informs the notion of human rights and other legal initiatives such as the 'common heritage of humankind' (embedded in the Law of the Sea (1982)), but it is not at the heart of the politics of sovereign states or corporate colossi; the principle of impartial moral reasoning might be appealed to to justify limits on reasons of state and the actions of IGOs, but it is, at best, only an incidental part of the institutional dynamics that have created such chronic political problems as the externalities (or border spillover effects) generated by many national economic and energy policies, overlapping communities of fate in areas as diverse as security and the environment, and the global polarization of power, wealth and income.

This should not be a surprise. In the first instance, the global legal and political initiatives of 1948 onwards do not just curtail sovereignty, they clearly support and underpin it in many ways. From the UN Charter to the Rio Declaration on the environment, international agreements have often served to entrench, and accommodate themselves to, the sovereign international power structure. The division of the globe into powerful nation-states, with distinctive sets of geopolitical interests, has often been built into the articles and statutes of IGOs.[32] The 'sovereign rights of states' are frequently affirmed alongside more cosmopolitan leanings. Moreover, while a case can be made that cosmopolitan principles are part of 'the working creed' of officials in some United Nations agencies such as the United Nations Children's Fund (UNICEF), the UN Educational, Scientific and Cultural Organization (UNESCO), and the World Health Organization (WHO), and NGOs such as Amnesty International, Save the Children and Greenpeace, they can scarcely be said to be constitutive of the conceptual world of most modern politicians, democratic or otherwise.[33]

Second, the cosmopolitan reach of contemporary regional and global law rarely comes with a commitment to establish institutions with the resources and clout to make declared cosmopolitan intentions and objectives effective. The susceptibility of the UN to the agendas of the most powerful states, the partiality of many of its enforcement operations (or lack of them altogether), the underfunding of its organizations, the continued dependency of its programmes on financial support from a few major states, the weaknesses of the policing of many environmental regimes (regional and global) are all indicative of the disjuncture between cosmopolitan aspirations and their partial and one-sided application. Cosmopolitan theory, with its emphasis on illegitimate structures of power and vital need, has to be reconnected to cosmopolitan institution-building. We require a shift from a club-driven and executive-led multilateralism – which is typically secretive and exclusionary – to a more transparent, accountable and just form of governance: a socially backed, cosmopolitan multilateralism.[34]

Cosmopolitan multilateralism

Cosmopolitan multilateralism takes as its starting point a world of 'overlapping communities of fate'. Recognizing the complex structures of an interconnected world, it views certain issues as appropriate for spatially delimited political spheres (the city, state or region), while it sees others – such as the environment, world health and economic regulation – as requiring new, more extensive institutions to address them. Deliberative and decision-making centres beyond national territories are appropriately situated when the cosmopolitan principles of equal worth, reciprocal recognition and impartial treatment can only be properly redeemed in a transnational context; when those significantly affected by a public matter constitute a cross-border or transnational grouping; and when 'lower' levels of decision-making cannot manage and discharge satisfactorily transnational or international policy questions. Only a cosmopolitan political outlook can ultimately accommodate itself to the political challenges of a more global era, marked by transnational externalities, overlapping communities of fate and growing global inequalities.

A cosmopolitan polity can only be satisfactorily entrenched if a division of powers and competencies is recognized at different levels of political action and interconnectedness – levels which correspond to the degrees to which public issues stretch across borders and significantly affect diverse populations. Such a polity must embrace diverse and distinct domains of authority, linked both vertically and horizontally, if it is to be a successful servant of cosmopolitan principles and practices. Of course, the boundaries demarcating different levels of governance will always be contested, as they are, for example, in existing local, subnational regional and national polities. Disputes about the appropriate jurisdiction for handling particular public issues will be complex and intensive; but better complex and intensive in a clear public framework than simply left to powerful geopolitical interests (dominant states) or market-based organizations to resolve them alone.

The possibility of a cosmopolitan polity must be linked to an expanding framework of states and agencies bound by, and committed to, cosmopolitan principles and rules. How should this be understood from an institutional point of view? To begin with, the possibility of cosmopolitan politics would be enhanced if the UN system actually lived up to the UN Charter. Among other things, this would mean pursuing measures to implement key elements of rights Conventions, and enforcing the prohibition on the discretionary right to use force.[35] In addition, if the Charter framework were extended – for example, by providing means of redress in the case of human rights violations, or by modifying the veto arrangement in the Security Council and rethinking representation on it to allow for adequate regional accountability – a basis might be established for the UN Charter system to generate political resources of its own, and to act as an autonomous decision-making centre – an important step towards establishing and maintaining cosmopolitan values, human rights and the rule of law in international affairs.

However, while each move in this direction would be significant, it would still represent, at best, a move towards a very incomplete form of accountability and justice in global politics. For the dynamics and logic of the current hierarchical interstate system (with the US in pole position) would still represent an immensely powerful force in global affairs; the massive disparities of power and asymmetries of resources in the global political economy would be left virtually unaddressed; ad hoc responses to pressing international and transnational issues would remain typical; there would be no forum for the pursuit of global questions directly accountable to the subjects and agencies of civil societies; and the whole question of the accountability of international organizations and global bodies would remain unresolved.

Thus, linked with the changes already described, a cosmopolitan polity would need to entrench an overarching network of public fora, covering cities, nation-states, regions and the wider global order. People would come to enjoy membership in diverse communities which significantly affect them, and would have access to a variety of forms of political engagement. It is possible to conceive of different types of political engagement on a continuum from the local to the global, with the local marked by direct and participatory processes while larger domains with significant populations are progressively mediated by representative mechanisms. The possibilities for direct involvement in the public affairs of small communities are clearly more extensive compared to those which exist in highly differentiated social, economic and political circumstances.[36] However, the simple juxtaposition of participatory with representative democracy is now in flux given developments in information technology, which put simultaneous two-way communication within reach of larger populations;[37] stakeholder innovations in democratic representation, which emphasize the significance of the direct involvement of representatives of all major groupings affected by a public process, instead of all the individuals involved;[38] and new approaches in deliberative democracy which do not take citizens' interests and preferences as simply pre-set, and seek to create accessible, diverse fora for the examination of opinion and informed participation.[39] The latter can be thought of as public spheres in which collective views and decisions are arrived at through deliberation – deliberation which is guided by the test of impartiality, as opposed to that of simple self-interest, in the formation of political will and judgement.

Accordingly, a cosmopolitan polity would seek the creation of an effective and accountable administrative, legislative and executive capacity at regional and global levels to *complement* those at local and national levels. This would require the following:

(1) The creation of regional parliaments and governance structures (for example, in Latin America and Africa), and the enhancement of the role of such bodies where they already exist (the European Union) in order that their decisions become recognized and accepted as legitimate independent sources of regional and international regulation. The focus would be on region-wide problems and challenges which states alone cannot resolve.

(2) The establishment of an authoritative assembly of all democratic states and agencies. This could take the form of a reformed General Assembly of the United Nations, or a complement to it. The focus of a global assembly would be the examination of those pressing problems which are at the heart of the possibility of the implementation of cosmopolitan principles – for instance, health

and disease, food supply and distribution, the debt burden of the developing world, the instability of the hundreds of billions of dollars that circulate the globe daily, global warming and the reduction of the risks of nuclear, chemical and biological warfare. Its task would be to set down the rules, standards and institutions required to embed cosmopolitan values and priorities. The instruments at its disposal would need to include framework-setting law, law which specified and articulated the core concerns of cosmopolitanism.[40] Consistent with this would be capacities to initiate attempts to alleviate crises of urgent need generating immediate life and death considerations. If non-global levels of governance were failing to protect people in these circumstances, a *raison d'être* would exist for direct global intervention. Of course, political decision-making and implementation should remain, everything else being equal, as much as possible with those who are primarily affected by them, in line with the principle of subsidiarity.[41]

Agreement on the terms of reference of a global assembly would be difficult to say the least, although there is no shortage of plausible schemes and models.[42] Ultimately, its terms of reference and operating rules would need to command widespread agreement and, hence, ought to be generated in a stakeholder process of consensus-building – a global constitutional convention – involving states, IGOs, INGOs, citizen groups and social movements. A global process of consultation and deliberation, organized at diverse levels, represents the best hope of creating a legitimate framework for accountable and sustainable global governance.

(3) The opening up of functional international governmental organizations (such as the WTO, IMF and World Bank) to public examination and agenda setting. Not only should such bodies be transparent in their activities, but they should be accessible and open to public scrutiny (on the basis perhaps of elected supervisory bodies, or functional delegative councils representative of the diverse interests in their constituencies), and accountable to

regional and global democratic fora (see points 1 and 2 above). In addition, where IGOs are currently weak and/or lacking in enforcement capability, new mechanisms and organizations need to be established, for example in the areas of the environment and social affairs. The creation of new global governance structures with responsibility for addressing poverty, welfare and related issues is vital to offset the power and influence of market-orientated agencies such as the WTO and IMF.

(4)   The staging of general referenda, in the case of contested priorities concerning the implementation of core cosmopolitan concerns, that cut across nations and nation-states at regional or global levels.[43] These could involve many different kinds of referenda, including a cross-section of the public, and/or of targeted and significantly affected groups in a particular policy area, and/or of the policy-makers and legislators of national parliaments. The use of referenda, and the establishment of the democratic accountability of international organizations, would involve people in issues which profoundly affect them but which – in the context of the current lacunae and fragmentation of international organizations – inevitably seem remote.

(5)   The development of a cosmopolitan law-enforcement and coercive capability, including peacekeeping and peace-making. It is necessary to meet the concern that, in the face of the pressing and violent challenges to cosmopolitan values and priorities, 'covenants, without the sword, are but words' (Hobbes). One of the enduring lessons of the twentieth century and the opening stages of the twenty-first must surely be that human progress remains an extraordinarily fragile achievement. Without the means of law enforcement, the institutional framework for a new cosmopolitan order cannot be properly conceived. On the other hand, only to the extent that the new forms of military arrangement are locked into a cosmopolitan framework would there be good grounds for

thinking that a new settlement could be created between coercive power and accountability.

To meet these objectives, a proportion of a nation-state's military could be 'seconded' to the new regional or global authorities and, once moulded into coherent units, placed at their disposal on a routine footing; or, better still, these authorities could establish enforcement capabilities of their own, creating a permanent independent force recruited directly from among individuals who volunteer from all countries. The restraints on the use of this force would have to be clearly delineated; the use of force should always be thought of as a collective option of last resort. The deployment of force could be justified, after all other forms of negotiation and sanction have been exhausted, only in the context of a serious threat to cosmopolitan institutions by state or non-state actors, to human rights by tyrannical regimes, or to peoples in circumstances which spiral beyond their control (such as the violent disintegration of a state).

Political cosmopolitanism involves the development of administrative capacity and independent political resources at regional and global levels as a necessary complement to those in local and national polities. At issue is strengthening the administrative capacity and accountability of regional institutions like the EU along with developing administrative capacity and forms of accountability at the level of the UN system itself. A cosmopolitan polity does not call for a diminution *per se* of state power and capacity across the globe. Rather, it seeks to entrench and develop political institutions at regional and global levels as a necessary complement to those at the level of the state. This conception of politics is based on the recognition of the continuing significance of nation-states, while arguing for layers of governance to address broader and more global questions. The aim is to forge an accountable and responsive politics at local and national levels alongside the establishment of representative and deliberative assemblies in the wider global order; that is, a political order of transparent and democratic cities and states as well as of regions and global networks.

The institutional requirements of political cosmopolitanism include:

- multilayered governance and diffused authority;
- a network of democratic fora from the local to the global;
- enhancing the transparency, accountability and effectiveness of leading functional IGOs, and building new bodies of this type where there is a demonstrable need for greater public coordination and administrative capacity;
- use of diverse forms of mechanisms to access public preferences, test their coherence and inform public will formation;
- establishment of an effective, accountable, international police/ military force for last resort use of coercive power in defence of cosmopolitan law.

Table 6.1 summarizes some ideal typical differences between executive and cosmopolitan multilateralism.

Conclusion: pie in the sky?

In the twentieth century political power was reshaped and reconfigured. It became diffused below, above and alongside the nation-state. Political power is multilevel and multilayered. Globalization has brought large swathes of the world's population 'closer together' in overlapping communities of fate. Life chances are affected by national, international and transnational processes. Cosmopolitan values are entrenched in important sectors of international law and new regional and global courts have been set up to examine some of the more heinous crimes humans can commit. Transnational movements, agencies and corporations have established the first stages of a global civil society. These and related developments create anchors for the development of a cosmopolitan

Executive *to* Cosmopolitan Multilateralism

Table 6.1 Ideal types of multilateralism

	Executive	Cosmopolitan
Organizational principle	Intergovernmentalism and geopolitics	Multilayered governance, multilevel authority
		Democratic deliberation, stakeholder representation (public and private), and impartiality as regulative ideals
Organizational interests	Particular state interests, accommodation to interstate and geoeconomic system	State interests, global civil society coalitions, environmental sustainability ('the common heritage of humankind')
Mode of organization	Secrecy, efficiency, statecraft, diplomatic interchange, geopolitical bargaining	Transparency, effectiveness, accountability and intergroup coordination and bargaining
Mode of voting	Eclectic; from weighted voting by financial muscle (IMF, World Bank), geopolitical strength (UN Security Council) to consensus (WTO)	Eclectic; from majority rule to consensus – depending on types of issue involved
Legitimacy	Reasons of state, state consent, world order values	Democratic legitimacy, social justice, and environmental protection

multilateralism. The latter does not have to start from scratch, but can develop from clear legal, political and civil stepping stones laid down in the twentieth century.

There are, of course, many reasons for pessimism. Globalization has not just integrated peoples and nations, but created new forms of antagonism and conflict. The globalization of communications does not just make it easier to establish mutual understanding, but often highlights what it is that people do not have in common and how and why differences matter. The dominant political game in the 'transnational town' remains geopolitics, and the one key player (the US) currently wants to rewrite the rules to further suit its hand. Ethnic self-centredness, right-wing nationalism and unilateralist politics are once again on the rise, and not just in the West. Yet the circumstances and nature of politics have changed. Like national culture and traditions, cosmopolitanism is a cultural and political project, but with one difference: it is better adapted and suited to our regional and global age. However, the arguments in support of this have yet to be fully established in the public sphere in many parts of the world; and we fail here at our peril.

It is important in conclusion to return to 9/11 and to say what it means in this context (cf. Keohane in this volume). One cannot accept the burden of putting accountability and justice right in one realm of life – physical security and political cooperation among defence establishments – without at the same time seeking to put it right elsewhere. If the political and the security, the social and the economic dimensions of accountability and justice are separated in the long term – as is the tendency in the global order today – the prospects of a peaceful and civil society will be bleak indeed. Popular support against terrorism, as well as against political violence and exclusionary politics of all kinds, depends upon convincing people that there is a legal, responsive and specific way of addressing their grievances. Without this sense of confidence in public institutions the defeat of terrorism and intolerance becomes a hugely difficult task, if it can be achieved at all. Globalization without cosmopolitanism could fail.

Against the background of 9/11, the current unilateralist stance of the US and the desperate cycle of violence in the Middle East and elsewhere, the advocacy of cosmopolitanism may appear like an attempt to defy gravity or walk on water! And, indeed, if it was a case of having to adopt cosmopolitan principles and institutions all at once, or not at all, this would be true. But it is no more the case than was the pursuit of the modern state – as a system of circumscribed authority, separate from ruler and ruled – at the time of Bodin and Hobbes. They worked in the context of a profound legacy of civil and religious strife in Europe; the advocacy of sovereign authority and an 'artificiall person' could have been dismissed as utopian. Yet there were foundations on which to build this edifice and political agents who, unable not to learn, could begin to reflexively reconstitute their political environment. Some two hundred years later the modern state became the dominant form of political organization, in Europe and later elsewhere. Of course, this achievement remains fragile in parts of the world, and the development of state capacity is an urgent task in many vulnerable countries. However, this project today is insufficient to create effective administration, the rule of law, accountability and justice; in a global age, political capacity has to be built elsewhere as well. For the last several decades the growth of multilateralism and the development of international law has created cosmopolitan anchors to the world. These are the basis for the further consolidation of the hold of cosmopolitan principles and institutions. Political and economic globalization creates the circumstances of cosmopolitanism; it remains for us to grasp them fully, now and in the future. In the current period, cosmopolitanism is a less utopian project than that set out by the theory of the modern state at the time of Hobbes's *Leviathan*.

Notes

1   D. Held and A. McGrew, D. Goldblatt and J. Perraton, *Global Transformations: Politics, Economics and Culture* (Cambridge:

Polity, 1999); D. Held and A. McGrew (eds), *The Global Transformations Reader* (Cambridge: Polity, 2000); D. Held and A. McGrew, *Globalization/Anti-Globalization* (Cambridge: Polity, 2002); D. Held, 'Law of states, law of peoples', *Legal Theory*, 8 (2002), pp. 1–44.

2   A. Giddens, *The Consequences of Modernity* (Cambridge: Polity, 1990), ch. 2.
3   See Held et al., *Global Transformations*, chs 1, 2 and 8.
4   I. Kaul, I. Grunberg and M. Stern (eds), *Global Public Goods: International Cooperation in the Twenty-First Century* (Oxford: Oxford University Press, 1999), pp. xixff.
5   These figures are drawn from the US economic census (1997) and from www.wwflearning.co.uk/news/features_0000000354.asp.
6   See Union of International Associations, *Yearbook of International Organizations 1996–7* (Munich: K. G. Saur, 1997).
7   Held et al., *Global Transformations*, chs 1–2.
8   I. Clark, *The Post Cold War Order* (Oxford: Oxford University Press, 2001).
9   Held et al., *Global Transformations*, ch. 2.
10   W. Wallace, 'The sharing of sovereignty: the European paradox?', *Political Studies*, 47 (1999).
11   P. Norris, 'Global governance and cosmopolitan citizens', in J. S. Nye and J. D. Donahue (eds), *Governance in a Globalizing World* (Washington DC: Brookings Institution Press, 2000), p. 175.
12   B. Barry, 'Statism and nationalism: a cosmopolitan critique', in I. Shapiro and L. Brilmayer (eds), *Global Justice* (New York: New York University Press, 1999), p. 35.
13   D. Held, *Democracy and the Global Order: From the Modern State to Cosmopolitan Governance* (Cambridge: Polity, 1995), ch. 10.
14   See Held, 'Law of states, law of peoples'.
15   See, for example, J. Waldron, 'What is cosmopolitan?', *Journal of Political Philosophy*, 8 (2000), and Barry, 'Statism and nationalism'.
16   H. G. Gadamer, *Truth and Method* (London: Sheed and Ward, 1975).
17   The following account of cosmopolitanism draws on sections of my 'Globalization, corporate practice and cosmopolitan social standards', *Contemporary Political Theory*, 1 (2002), pp. 59–78.
18   C. Beitz, 'Cosmopolitan liberalism and the states system', in C. Brown (ed.), *Political Restructuring in Europe: Ethical Perspectives*

(London: Routledge, 1994); C. Beitz, 'Philosophy of international relations', in *Routledge Encyclopedia of Philosophy* (London: Routledge, 1998); T. Pogge, 'Cosmopolitanism and sovereignty', in Brown, *Political Restructuring in Europe*.

19   A. Kuper, 'Rawlsian global justice: beyond *The Law of Peoples* to a cosmopolitan law of persons', *Political Theory*, 28 (2000), pp. 640–74.

20   Pogge, 'Cosmopolitanism and sovereignty', pp. 89f.

21   Ibid., p. 90.

22   O. O'Neill, 'Transnational justice', in D. Held (ed.), *Political Theory Today* (Cambridge: Polity, 1991).

23   B. Barry, *Theories of Justice* (London: Harvester Wheatsheaf, 1989); cf. T. M. Scanlon, *What We Owe to Each Other* (Cambridge, Mass.: Belknap, 1998).

24   T. Hill, 'The importance of autonomy', in E. Kittay and D. Meyers (eds), *Women and Moral Theory* (Totowa, N.J.: Rowman and Allanheld, 1987), p. 132, quoted in B. Barry, *Justice as Impartiality* (Oxford: Clarendon Press, 1995), pp. 226–7.

25   M. C. Nussbaum, 'Kant and cosmopolitanism', in J. Bohman and M. Lutz-Bachmann (eds), *Perpetual Peace* (Cambridge, Mass.: MIT Press, 1997), pp. 29–36.

26   See A. Sen, *Development as Freedom* (Oxford: Oxford University Press, 1999).

27   See Held, 'Law of states, law of peoples'.

28   J. Habermas, *Between Facts and Norms: Contributions to a Discourse Theory of Law and Democracy* (Cambridge: Polity, 1996).

29   See UN, *Human Rights: A Compilation of International Instruments* (New York: United Nations, 1988).

30   See M. Weller, 'The reality of the emerging universal constitutional order: putting the pieces together', *Cambridge Review of International Studies*, 10 (1997), pp. 40–63; J. Crawford and S. Marks, 'The global democracy deficit: an essay on international law and its limits', in D. Archibugi, D. Held and M. Köhler (eds), *Re-imagining Political Community* (Cambridge: Polity, 1998).

31   See Held, 'Law of states, law of peoples', for a survey.

32   See Held, *Democracy and the Global Order*, chs 5, 6.

33   Barry, 'Statism and nationalism', pp. 34–5; cf. Held and McGrew, *The Global Transformations Reader*, pp. 31–9.

34 I am indebted to Michael Zürn's distinction between 'executive' and 'social' multilateralism, which he made at a presentation at the London School of Economics, 17 May 2002.

35 See R. Falk, *On Humane Governance* (Cambridge: Polity, 1995).

36 See Held, *Democracy and the Global Order*, chs 7 and 9; see also D. Beetham, 'Liberal democracy and the limits of democratization', and A. Philips, 'Must feminists give up on liberal democracy?', both in D. Held (ed.), *Prospects for Democracy: North, South, East, West* (Cambridge: Polity, 1993).

37 I. Budge, 'Direct democracy: setting appropriate terms of debate', in Held, *Prospects for Democracy*.

38 J. Burnheim, *Is Democracy Possible?* (Cambridge: Polity, 1985); W. Hutton, *The World We're In* (London: Little, Brown, 2002).

39 J. Cohen, 'Deliberation and democratic legitimacy', in A. Hamlin and P. Pettit (eds), *The Good Polity* (Oxford: Blackwell, 1989); J. Fishkin, *Democracy and Deliberation* (New Haven: Yale University Press, 1991); Habermas, *Between Facts and Norms*.

40 European law embodies a range of relevant distinctions among legal instruments and types of implementation which it would be helpful to reflect on in this context; see T. C. Hartley, *The Foundations of European Law* (Oxford: Clarendon Press, 1988); J. Pinder, *European Community* (Oxford: Oxford University Press, 1992); L. Hooghe and G. Marks, *Multi-level Governance and European Integration* (Lanham, Md: Rowman and Littlefield, 2001).

41 Held, 'Law of states, law of peoples'.

42 See, for example, J. Segall, 'Building world democracy through the UN', *Medicine and War*, 6 (1990); J. Segall, 'A UN second assembly', in F. Barnaby (ed.), *Building a More Democratic United Nations* (London: Lass, 1991); Archibugi, Held and Köhler, *Re-imagining Political Community*, esp. chs 9, 10, 14 and 15.

43 Held, *Democracy and the Global Order*, ch. 12.

Index

Index

Bobbio, Norberto 4
Bodin, Jean 183
Boeuf Rouge Group 84
Bolivia 50–1
Botswana 47
Brazil 29, 49
Britain 98
Bull, Hedley 134, 138
Bush, George W.: debt crises 49; fast-track trade negotiation 100; rejects Kyoto Protocol 116

California and Nike lawsuit 109
Canada 102–3
capitalism: and capital flight 38–9; ethical investment 114; pitfalls of liberalization 58–61 *see also* multinational corporations
Castles, Ian 44*n*
certification institutions 108–10, 125*n*
China: compared to Russia 61; currency market 25; as globalizing nation 30–1, 41; income gaps 40; inequalities 96; own pace of liberalization 52; poverty 20, 22–3; purchasing power 26, 27, 28–9; research and development 38; skilled workers 34
civil society: and debt 52–3; embedded global economy 95; global public domain 114–16, 117; and multinational corporations 13
civil society organizations (CSO) 123*n*; role of 104–6
The Clash of Civilizations (Huntington) 157*n*

Clean Clothes Campaign 110
Clinton, Bill 61
communication: cosmopolitan identity 166–7; immediate and global 162; transnational flow of 2
Confederation of Independent States 25
copyright and patents: intellectual property 57
corporations: brand vulnerability 127*n*; codes of conduct 108–10; and 'corporatism' 117; and the environment 128–9*n*; social responsibility 95, 115 *see also* multinational corporations
cosmopolitanism: administration of polity 176, 181; in context of 9/11 182–3; definition and principles of 167–71; and democratic representation 175–6, 181; institution-building 171–3; law enforcement 178–9; legislating a polity 176–8, 181; legitimacy 181; multilateralism 173–80; self-identity and 166–7; utopia or possibility? 180–3
Côte d'Ivoire 30
crime: transnational issues of 162; in war/against humanity 171–2
currency *see* money and currencies

Deaton, Angus 20
debt: form of bankruptcy 64; IMF and Argentina 48–50; Jubilee Movement 52–3
democracy 66; and accountability 140–2; and cosmopolitanism

188

Index